LIFE

BEGINNING

RACHEL HAMM

Life Beginning

Copyright © 2017 Rachel Hamm

BOOK DEDICATION

To the one who encourages my wild dreams. To the one who's shown me the meaning of faithful and true. To the one who makes me feel like I'm the only woman in the world. To the one who helps me keep my feet on the ground just long enough to glue my broken garbage-can-lid-wings back together again. To my love, to Marshall. I can't imagine life without you. I adore you. You're simply the best thing that's ever happened to me... apart from Jesus, of course.

TABLE OF CONTENTS

Book Dedication 5

Introduction: Taste The Wild Honey 9

Chapter 1: You're Not Worth Celebrating 15

Chapter 2: Wildfires 28

Chapter 3: Baby Blue Caddy 39

Chapter 4: Break Time, Or Not 50

Chapter 5: Childhood Comes For Me At Night 65

Chapter 6: Every Little Part Of Me Is Going To Be OK 75

Chapter 7: Cloudy With A Chance Of Reign 90

Chapter 8: Meeting Father John 111

Chapter 9: Heavenly Lights 125

Chapter 10: I'm Back, Now What? 132

Chapter 11: I Like Him 140

Chapter 12: Medicate Me, Please 150

Chapter 13: Visions Of Babies Danced In His Head 168

Chapter 14: Don't Have Your Feelings Hurt, Silly Girl 177

Chapter 15: Diving Into The Deep 182

"For those who have ears to hear," He said.

"Yes, for those," I agreed. It is indeed a high price to pay. Some-times the cost of getting the wild honey is the isolation that comes with hammering out one's own course. Other times it's the bee stings that you endure. The stings swell and surge. They itch and cause so much discomfort.

I thought about how comfortable people like to be and felt dis-couraged. The love of comfort might keep many inexperienced in the ways of wild honey. The stings were painful and sometimes disfigured my face. I became unrecognizable, even to myself. I've encountered many bees, and I've been stung too many times to count. God alone knew *exactly* how many stings there had been.

Bee stings hurt; but in spite of the pain and disfigurement, the sweetness of the honey has been worth it. Don't take my word for it. Taste it, and decide for yourself. Merely hearing about it will not satisfy. Each person must taste for himself, if he's willing to pay the price. Some won't be. Plenty have made their comfortable couch their god. But for *those who will*...Come, taste the wild honey.

Me and Rich, The Honey Man

Endnote:

1 Urban, Keith Lionel, and Monty Powell. "These are the Days." Recorded 2004. Capitol Records Nashville.

CHAPTER 1

CHAPTER 1

You're Not Worth Celebrating

I Love Jesus, But...

In a desperate search for levity I was watching a talk show one afternoon. While on air, the hostess called an elderly woman named Gladys from Austin, Texas. Gladys had called the show's studio and left a voicemail to let her know she needed to move some plants. Apparently, the plants on the studio set were placed in such a way that it looked like they were growing out of the hostess' head. The hostess called to thank Gladys for her suggestion and to see if she had any others. In the middle of their conversation, Gladys stopped mid-sentence and told the hostess, "Listen, I'll be honest with you. I love Jesus, but I drink a little."

After I finished laughing at Gladys, the straight shooter, I thought, *I love this woman!* I love people who tell the truth, even when it makes them look bad. I could relate to Gladys! I love Jesus, but I drink a little. I love Jesus, but I've battled depression and anxiety. I love Jesus, but my house was foreclosed. I love Jesus, but I've got an ego that I shouldn't have. I love Jesus, but I've got "issues" and plenty of them. I love Jesus, but I've often been rejected by His followers. I wonder what you would put in that blank? I love Jesus, but...?

Misperception

I love Jesus, but I was conceived outside the confines of wedlock. In the mid-seventies that was still a dishonorable way to enter the world, and the church my parents were members of made sure that they knew it. You know, lest they accidentally forget. The church leadership informed my mom they would *not* be throwing her a baby shower. After all, her baby had been conceived in sin. They threw showers for all the other expectant mothers who'd done things in the proper order, but not for my mom.

The way the church handled that situation caused there to be a shameful label on me. As I grew I *felt* it. I felt like a second-class citizen because of the way my life began. Once something like shame takes root, it can be tough to gain freedom. I felt like the church was saying, "Because of your parents' sin, *you're* not worth celebrating." Whether or not that's what they meant, that's the message I perceived, and you know what they say about perception: Perception is reality.

Perhaps they did this to...teach my parents a lesson. Perhaps if they humiliated my parents, it would scare other teens into remaining celibate. Perhaps it's a simpler reason: my parents sinned and they needed to be punished. I'm not certain *why* that church did what they did, but I am certain of how it made me feel.

Even now, as I think about their actions it makes my stomach burn; I feel tense and hollow, I feel like tipping my head towards my feet, feel like I should sit in the back of the bus, and like my whole existence is an intolerable, sinful mistake.

Thanks, Frank

Fast forward 35 years from my birth. I live in California, and I called my spiritual mentor Snow, who lives in Tennessee. I was making some big decisions and needed wisdom. As we talked, Snow said, "I'm being led to have you call this man I know so he can pray for you. He's very wise. He spends his days in prayer, and he loves to pray for people over the phone. He lives in Idaho, and his name is Frank. I'm going to give you his phone number, okay?" (By "being led" Snow meant she believed God was directing her to do this.)

"Um, okay,...*I guess*. I don't want to bother him since I don't even know him. Could *you* just pray for me, Snow?" She assured me I would not be bothering him. "He loves praying for people, and often God will show Him things on your behalf." She said he was a mighty man of God, and I would be blessed by talking to him. She would not be praying for me. I needed to call Frank in Idaho.

With a decent amount of reluctance, I called. And she was right. I loved Frank from Idaho. He had a sweet, tender spirit. His voice was calm and kind, and talking to him was indeed a blessing. I told him Snow suggested I call, and he said he was glad I had. He prayed for me, and God did show him some things about my life. He said some powerful things to me that day that gave me hope. He prophesied over my future, and I felt my spine straightening out as he did.

After he was done praying and ministering to me, he asked me how I knew Snow. I told him our families had been friends for decades starting in Central California. My grandparents had been friends with Snow's family, and then my parents, and now me. He said, "Central California? I used to live in Central California! Who are your parents and grandparents?" I told him their names, and there was silence. Then, loud, hearty laughter came roaring through the phone. "Well, Rachel, I know *you*."

"You know *me*?"

"Yes, ma'am. I know *you*. I knew you before you were born. My wife and I threw your mama and daddy a baby shower in our home when your mama was pregnant with you. Yes, indeed, I do know *you*. Rachel....Rachel Roberts, you sweet thing. It is so good to hear your voice, all grown up. Well, Lord, I do thank You for letting me meet back up with sweet little Rachel today! Yes, I do thank You for this gift. Thank You for the *gift of Rachel*.

Now, Rachel, when your mama was pregnant with you, there were some nasty people in the church who thought they were better than everyone else. You know the type? Nobody likes those kinds of people. My wife and I knew there was going to be something very special about you, Miss Rachel. God had shown us we were to throw you a baby shower and honor your life, because you, Darling, were going to be very special. And, yes, I can see now you *are* so special! Wow, well, I'll be darned, little Rachel Roberts!" More hearty laughter from Frank.

A lump formed in my throat as I realized what this man and his wife had done for me before I was born. Throwing my mom a baby shower was kind and righteous. Hearing about what they had done made my head turn upward towards the horizon. It made my stomach feel less hollow and tense. It made me feel like I should move to the front of the bus. I felt like maybe, just maybe, my life really mattered.

Tears rolled down my cheeks as this dear elderly man who'd defied the church leaders all those years ago was now praying and ministering life to me yet again. I marveled at the fact God brought us together that day on the phone, despite many states and years separating us. He was a stranger to me, but God knew. I thought about how God had set up this "wild honey" situation for Frank and me. How pleased He must have been to see us tasting it that day.

When Frank said God had shown him and his wife there was something special about me even *before I was born*, I felt part of my shame label fall to the ground. I chose to believe if God had shown them that before I was born, maybe my coat of many contemptible colors really didn't belong to me after all. Maybe my shame was a case of mistaken identity.

The yin and the yang of life...I've seen it over and over. Shame, and then the restoration of dignity. The hateful act and then the loving, generous gesture. The rejection and the acceptance. Condemnation from the church leaders, and then the prophetic esteeming from Frank, and it's mixed together swirling all around us. That's life. Well, that's been *my* life.

Yin and Yang

I've walked an arduous and winding road as I've pursued the spiritual life. As hard as I try to keep my filthy feet on the ground, I can't seem to keep my mind from floating up towards the cotton candy sky. I have an insatiable appetite for the deep things of God. From the tiniest of age, I found myself enthralled with God, Jesus, and The Holy Spirit. They've captured my attention and affection, and I've found Them to be the most fascinating and captivating subjects that I think about. I can't seem to quench my desire to see God, to understand who He is, and to perceive His activity pulsating in the world in and around me. For the first 37 years of my life, I only looked for Him in churches, but kept accidentally finding Him everywhere else. Now I just look for Him wherever I find myself at any given moment.

I've had the most beautiful, fascinating, miraculous spiritual experiences outside the four walls of a church building. These encounters have often come through the most unusual and unlikely sources. They've often come through people that I'd secretly discounted or tried to avoid. I've had these amazing experiences with Jesus because of His followers and even in spite of them.

I've had an unusually high amount of experiences with the dark side of the spiritual spectrum as well. I've been in places where evil plans were being implemented and have seen the dark side of humanity in a way that is uncommon. I've had many highs, and I've had many lows. The worst things that I've been through were at the hands of "Christians," or at least that's what they called themselves. Be wary of believing someone is a Christian just because he says he is. When someone tells you he's a Christian...as they say, "The proof is in the pudding." Here is how Jesus said it:

Watch out for false teachers. They come to you dressed as if they were sheep. On the inside they are hungry wolves. You will know them by their fruit. Do men pick grapes from thorns? Do men pick figs from thistles? It is true, every good tree has good fruit. Every bad tree has bad fruit. A good tree cannot have bad fruit. A bad tree cannot have good fruit. Every tree that does not have good fruit is cut down and thrown into the fire. So you will know them by their fruit. Not everyone who says to me, 'Lord, Lord,' will go into the holy nation of heaven. The one who does the things My Father in heaven wants him to do will go into the holy nation of heaven. Many people will say to Me on that day, "Lord, Lord, did we not preach in Your Name? Did we not put out demons in Your Name? Did we not do many powerful works in Your Name?" Then I will say to them in plain words, "I never knew you. Go away from Me, you who do wrong."
(Matthew 7:15-23)

We'd be wise to heed Jesus' warning here. Darkness tries to disguise itself in light, so we must be alert and shrewd. The hard part is that the wolves are milling around wearing sheep costumes. They're grazing with the genuine sheep. Lord, give us eyes to discern the difference between wool and cotton balls.

Just to be clear, I go to church. I love my church. I'm not bashing the church in general. I've got issues with darkness that's masquerading as light. I *am* bashing *that*! I am bashing the religious spirit that I've encountered in many churches. I am bashing the box that God has been put in. I am bashing shepherds that are stealing the sheep's food and allowing wolves access to those they are called to protect. Just to be clear.

Throughout my life God has shown me supernatural phenomenon, given me special gifts and miracles, and His unyielding, all-encompassing, demonstrative love. Satan has simultaneously sought to humiliate me, kill me, drive me insane, and cause me to be rejected by my church multiple times. The yin and yang of my life has been dramatic.

The Con Artist

Towards the end of my first-grade year my family was moving *again*. At the age of six, I was being enrolled in my *fourth* elementary school. When you move as much as I did, you develop an uncanny ability to adapt. I learned how to read people, and learned how I could reinvent myself to fit into each new environment.

At this new school I met Elise. She had long, brown wavy hair, green eyes, and lots of freckles. She was kind and good-natured, and seemed like someone I could be friends with. I set out to discover what interested her so I could adjust myself accordingly and be put on her friend list. She liked karate, and I'd seen karate in an episode of "Scooby Doo," so I was pretty confident I knew enough about it to trick her into thinking it was my thing too. She'd explained to me there were different-colored belts and there was a ladder you could climb until you reached black belt. I said I, of course, knew that already. I then tucked that information about karate in the back of my own black belt until the day that I was invited to go to her house to play.

I arrived at Elise's house, and her mom was tall and pretty, just like Elise. I liked her, and I wanted her to like me too. Hoping to impress her, I brought up the subject of karate. "Did you know I'm in karate too, just like Elise?"

"Oh, you are? No, I didn't know that. That's fantastic! It's a great set of skills for us girls to be learning!" *Us* girls? I thought. It turns out that Elise's mom had been in karate most of her life.

Much to my surprise she went on to say things about karate that had *not* been covered by the writers of "Scooby Doo"! Fearing my lie would be discovered, I thought I better switch to showing her some moves so she wouldn't think I was lying.

"Would you like to see some of my karate moves? I just became a black belt, so yeah, I'm *pretty good*!" I said with smug, deceitful, idiotic, arrogance.

With a large smile on her face, she said, "Oh, wow, okay, yes," as she sat down on her Asian-inspired couch to watch my Asian-inspired moves.

I then began creating karate-type moves and was kicking and chopping all over my new friends' living room. I went from one move right into the other, and I even gave the moves names. She laughed and laughed and laughed as I did my fake karate moves and used a bunch of bogus karate lingo. I knew her laughter came from a deep sense of joy that she'd found a fellow karate-loving comrade. I thought I looked like a pro, and I'd just blown the socks off these nice new friends. Success felt even more satisfying than I'd anticipated.

Optimistically, I strolled home that day thinking, "Nice, job, Rach!" There was only one, small problem with my attempt to con them: they were the real deal. They *really did* know all about karate. That was the only aspect of the scam I hadn't thought through. I could have gotten away with it if it weren't for their rascally knowledge. I *might* have been able *slightly* to fool someone who didn't know anything about karate, but I was acting like an idiot with people who knew all about it. They were legit. I was, well, not legit.

I won't even tell you about the other situation where I wore a Michael Jackson button on my denim jacket everyday so my African American teacher would feel like I supported "her people." Nor, how I told her, "My bedroom walls are *covered* with posters of black people because I *love* black people!" I figured wearing that button and telling her about my make-believe posters would grant me her approval. I was always trying to adjust myself to be acceptable to those around me. Maybe you've done the same at some point?

Jesus' Warning

Frank and his wife were legit. Those people who said my mom couldn't have a baby shower were, well, not legit. It was never Jesus' way to shame those caught in sin. He'd lovingly inspired them toward a better way. It's the love of God that leads people to repentance. He did, however, have pretty harsh words for the church leaders who were self-righteous. Jesus warned us about the kind of people we'd encounter:

Beware of wolves who will disguise themselves as sheep. (Matthew 7:15)

Beware of the Pharisees (self-righteous church leaders).

(Matthew 16:5-6, Matthew 3:7-10, Matthew 15:20)

He also told us that we'd be able to tell the kind of tree based on what kind of fruit it produces. (Matthew 7:16-21)

If a sheep has a lot of wolf-like tendencies, guess what? If a tree tells you it's a peach tree, but every year you see lemons hanging on those branches, guess what? Believing a lemon tree is actually a peach tree when it's producing lemons is as good an idea as Elise and her mom believing I was a black belt in karate. I'm not talking about Christians that are imperfect and struggling along toward holiness and sanctification. I'm talking about people who say they're Christians, but they're consistently turning out rotten fruit, year in and year out. It might be possible they're not really believers. Maybe you've been hurt by a Christian, who wasn't actually a Christian.

Have you ever come across people who said they were Christ-followers, but something about that proclamation just didn't add up? Have you ever been wounded by people who were claiming to follow The Healer? Ever been rejected by people who were supposedly following the most loving Man who ever walked the face of the earth? I hope you haven't. I hope you've always been accepted and cherished for who you *really* are, with no shame. I hope you've never been rejected because of your gender, social status, the color of your skin, your own sin, your parents' sin, or for any other reason. Because shame is *NOT* Jesus' way! Jesus is all about giving purpose, hope, dignity, healing, and truckloads of unconditional love. (See John 8:1-11.)

The Light

As I've been volleyed back and forth between good and evil I've discovered some treasures, a gold mine really. I've scouted the locations of the sweetest honeycombs you'll ever find. I've been healed from what the wolves in sheep's clothing have done to me and, in the process, I've learned some things. I've been shaped, I've grown, and I've acquired some jars of wild honey that have made the pain worth it. But I don't feel satisfied to have just gathered these things for myself. I now have a deep desire to share them with *you*. Learning, in and of itself, has some value, but the real gold comes from sharing what you've learned with others.

When you've been through hell, there's a comfort in knowing you've plundered the enemy's camp while you were there, taking enough for yourself *and others*. So many things that have been stolen from us are in the enemy's camp, and retrieving it feels amazing! When I was in hell, I begged God to bring justice to my scales. (I'll explain more of what I mean by saying "when I was in hell" in chapter 3.) I asked Him for redemption. His answer to my plea was a resounding "YES!" He's given me so many jewels, so many jars of honey, more than I asked for. That's just how God is. He gives us more than we ask or can even imagine (Ephesians 3:20), *but we do need to ask*. We don't want to "have not because we ask not." (See James 4:2-3.)

This book is a way to honor The Light that enveloped me when I was surrounded by snarling wolves. It's also a way of making evil pay for what he's done to me by way of those wolves. The words written on these pages are part of my redemptive process.

That Light that enveloped me has also been present with *you* in your darkest moments. We don't always see The Light with us, and the dark can feel so very dark. When I was in my healing process, Jesus began to show me He was with me in every single dark situation. That puzzled me, and I asked Him, "Why did those situations feel unbearably dark at the time? Why didn't I see Your presence of light in the middle of that dark?"

Jesus' response, "Because your eyes were closed. Sometimes pain makes us close our eyes. It's a way we protect ourselves, but the backs of closed eyelids are the darkest kind of dark. Because of the wounds that have come, many people are walking through life with their eyes closed. I'm right there with them, but they can't see Me."

As you read this book, I pray you'll be brave enough to open your eyes so you can see The Light. If your eyes are already open,

I pray you will step further into The Light as you read. As I present my life to you, may you see your own life in a whole new way. May you see God in a whole new way. Maybe as you read my story, you'll gain a deeper understanding about how God works *all* things together for our good. May you have the courage to see the good and the evil without looking away, and may your soul find the healing that it craves. When I opened my eyes and saw The Light, it healed me. It wasn't life-changing. It was life-beginning.

CHAPTER 2

Wildfires

They say that time's supposed to heal ya
But I ain't done much healing
Hello, can you hear me?
I'm in California dreaming about who we used to be
When we were younger [1]

In 2014 the summer heat snuck up on me like only things that originate in hell can do. California was experiencing a horrible drought. There'd been little to no rain for the last three years, and then came along our hot, dry, infernal summer heat. Wildfires were burning up much of the state's land, and the economy was in the toilet. Desperation and thirst were in the air and in my soul.

Along with wickedly high temperatures summer brought, for me, an emotional wildfire that was burning at breakneck speed and seemed to come out of nowhere. If I'd been accurately interpreting my dreams from January, February, March, April, and

May, the wildfire would have been no surprise but apparently, I was not. There were dreams of men chasing me, lost and stolen identity, countless betrayals, missed flights, dead babies, Keith Urban and Nicole Kidman, witches cursing me, Muslims massacring, houses, and fires, *lots of fires*. There were also visionary dreams from God thrown into the mix.

Just four months before hell's heat came to visit, I'd met a well-known prophetic man in Dallas, Texas. He was as handsome as he was wise. To me he was a spiritual giant, at five feet, nine inches. His white hair and beard were thick, as were the heels of his cowboy boots. His name was John Paul Jackson, and I'd flown to Dallas to take his class about dream interpretation. He was a spiritual genius, and I greatly admired him. When we met, his steel blue eyes looked deep into my bluish/green ones and he said, "After this trip, everything is going to change for you, *everything*. One year from now your life will be unrecognizable to you." In spite of my wildly creative imagination, I could *never* have guessed exactly what that meant.

Random side note and fun fact: A couple of days before I flew to Dallas, I had a dream about the class I'd be taking. I was hovering above the room where the class would be. I saw myself walk into the room and up to the front. I took a seat in the front row, third chair from the right. I sat next to a man who knew the instructor of the class, and then I woke up.

A few days later when I arrived at the class, that was the scene. I walked in and there was one empty seat in the front row, third seat from the right. I sat in that seat next to a man who was friends with the instructor. Because of their friendship, the instructor came and talked to that man during breaks, which allowed me to have some amazing conversations and get a lot of one-on-one time with the instructor. If you don't already, pay attention to your dreams!

Four months after meeting that handsome, prophetic Texan, my family was in the throes of our tenth move in seventeen years. That's right *tenth in seventeen!* This one was fairly happy. Not all of them had been. The move just prior to this one had been chalked with bitterness. This one was better, although not ideal. Being an idealist, I found this to be, well, not ideal. My husband had really wanted to move to this house, but I was not certain that it was best. He persisted, and I succumbed. This was a *rare* occasion where he was right, and I was wrong. (Just kidding, of course. As I've gotten older I've realized that my husband is very wise, and when I listen to his counsel things always go better. His wisdom is a beautiful gift.)

The temperatures scorched us as we moved into our new home. Moving is hard enough without the heat; with it, it's unbearable. We wiped our brows and pushed through. Immediately upon moving into this new house, a series of unusual events happened in one week's time. I'll get into the specifics of those later. For now, I'll just say those events led me into counseling for some trauma I'd never dealt with.

I was 37 years old, and I needed to deal with things that happened decades ago. There's a reason I'd not dealt with them before this time. It's *hard* to deal with hard things. If I could have handled dealing with this stuff any sooner, I would have. While I do *not* believe in the adage "Time heals everything," I do believe time can lessen the intensity of a traumatic experience.

I also believe time tends to produce a stability, strength and wisdom only years of living can bring. I'm not sure you can bypass the process of walking through some things and gaining wisdom and strength the old-fashioned way. I believe in a gift of wisdom and strength that comes supernaturally from God; but for the most part wisdom and strength are gained *slowly* through the long, *hard* years. I'd gained some wisdom through my own long, hard years so now, at this point, I could deal with... *really difficult things.*

Let's Heal, Shall We?

So, at the ripe old age of 37, I'd been through enough, learned enough, and was stable enough to handle processing *very difficult* things. My life was pretty good and reasonably healthy. However, I felt like I was hitting a wall, like I'd gone as far as I could go without dealing with my "stuff." Do you have experiences from the past you've stuffed down and tried to forget? Maybe a lot of us do, just to differing degrees? I certainly did, and I thought I'd done so with a reasonable amount of success. But then I got to a point where that wasn't good enough. I felt agitated and restless. Anaïs Nin said it this way:

> *"And the day came when the risk to remain tight in a bud was more painful than the risk it took to blossom."* [2]

That day came for me. I'd always thought that tight buds were pretty, but I began to see that once they fully bloomed they were even prettier. I'd experienced hardships and wounds, and I had to decide whether or not to deal with it all. Dealing with it would require thinking about it, and it was what I'd spent most of my life trying to forget. However, at some point those memories rise to the surface of our souls and sit staring at us, eye-to-eye. No matter how hard I tried to "keep the monsters down," they kept popping up again.

When monsters from our past pop up, we have to decide: are we going to stay in the bud or bloom? Eat, drink, distract, and medicate or take a bold look at the truth? I'll admit, blooming is not for the faint of heart. It requires uprooting weeds, examining and exterminating pests, fertilizing, and dealing with unhealthy roots.

I had so many blessings in my life. There'd been a lot of highs amidst the low moments. I'd tasted plenty of wild honey. However, there were wounds that just sat there, festering, in need of deep healing.

There is a high cost to healing and blooming. Some aren't willing to pay that price. Others simply don't know blooming is possible. They've been in a tight bud for so long they don't realize those petals were meant to open and lay in a relaxed, lovely layered position. Some are willing to bloom, but lack information and resources. As I talk with people, I've found many of us fall into the category of being too afraid to heal and bloom. There are too many unknowns in the process. The unknowns are fear invoking. Still others seem disinterested in healing, or feel they can't handle the cost of it. That makes me sad because it's not true.

He watched his life flash before his eyes in the middle of a hurricane.
Came out alive on the other side.
That's where the other side got its name. [3]

When you come out on the other side of the healing process, the result is so profound that you give that side a name. As someone who's on the backside of healing, I can tell you that the pain is worth the end result.

Let's Do This

In 2014 I concluded that the cost and risk of *not* blooming was worse than the alternative. So, I plunged into the rewarding, tiring, expensive process of blooming. That consisted of counseling that was the equivalent of ripping off full-body scabs and pouring rubbing alcohol on them, taking some scary steps, reporting someone who'd abused me, and being very, *very* brave.

Multiple times during counseling I asked my counselor, "Why is this worth it again?" She would remind me I would never be *fully free* and would never become *all* I was created to be if I didn't go into those secret, wounded places and wage war on the dark powers that resided there. In my gut I knew she was right, so I persisted in the rewarding, heartbreaking, illuminating endeavor.

As hard as the healing and blooming process was, there was a lot of relief that came in the middle of the pain. It was very freeing to give a voice to the hurting parts of my soul. It was surprisingly liberating to *finally* talk about the real-life nightmares I'd never spoken of. While in the counseling process, I felt truly known for the first time in my life. Until then I had no idea how much pain I was in due to not *truly* being known. I discovered there was not a soul on earth who really knew me...*including myself!* Zora Neale Hurston, said it this way, "There is no greater agony than bearing an untold story inside you." [4]

It's true that talking about the dark things I'd experienced brought on pain, but it simultaneously alleviated it. Healing is a strange, mixed bag of emotions. It's complex and hard and beautiful all at the same time. It's kind of like the best of times and the worst of times.

It's All You, Baby!

By August I was a couple of months into this process and my

heart was in pieces. I was tired and lonely. When you decide to go into the dark rooms of your soul, no one can *fully* go into them with you. As much as they love you and are there for you, you're alone and you know it. You *feel* it. Even when someone has been through something similar, no one has experienced your exact scenario. Friends who stick with you through the drudgery and ugliness are so appreciated, but as Billy Joel said, "Like a boxer in a title fight, you've got to walk into that ring all alone." [5]

You are the one, the only one, who can climb in, slide on those gloves, insert the mouthpiece, and start throwing punches. Healing is not exactly a team sport. Although The Healer, The Holy Spirit, never leaves you. His presence makes the process doable.

I'm being honest about the cost because I don't want to be one of those salesmen that downplays the cost of becoming the best, fullest, most peaceful, joyful version of yourself. Becoming emotionally healthy, going through counseling, and dealing with our demons is a lot of hard work. It's especially hard at the beginning, but it gets easier as you go. It's a high risk and a high reward, or low risk and low reward kind of situation. You get to choose.

I've personally taken the philosophy that if I'm going to live, I may as well *really* live. I don't want to just get through barely surviving. I want to thrive. I think that I'd do well in Texas with their "go big or go home" philosophy. We may as well give it all we've got. We only get one life.

While I'm not going to downplay the cost, I'm also not going to downplay how great the payoff is. Life is beautiful for the brave; and make no mistake about it, the brave choose healing! We could choose to ignore the dark things crawling around inside ourselves, *but not if we want to reach our highest destinies.*

The payoff is so small if we go down the path of least resistance, which does not lead to our healing. Not to mention the traffic on the avoid-pain-at-all-costs-and-don't-deal-with-hard-things-just-distract-yourself-with-busyness-or-medicate-the-pain path is terrible! There are a lot of people on that path. It's a crowded street, and I hate bad traffic. Don't you?

It's true that we won't be able to stay numb if we choose to face our demons and get healing. When we're no longer numb, we *do* feel pain; but don't be afraid of some pain. Be afraid of never becoming who you were created to be! Be afraid of standing before God and hearing Him say, "I had so much more for you, but fear kept you from it." Be afraid of *that!*

What if you haven't become the highest, best version of yourself because your main goal is to avoid pain? You might not be conscious of the fact that your main goal is to avoid pain, but for most people that's the case. We are motivated by two main things: the pursuit of pleasure and the avoidance of pain. Out of these two pursuits, humans will go to the greatest lengths to avoid pain. But often in order to achieve the *highest* form of pleasure, we must first endure some pain.

If you have wounds from your past, and if you deal with them (endure some pain), you could be catapulted from existing to flourishing (the highest form of pleasure). What if it were possible for you to go to The Healer's gate and with some courage, counsel, and a willing heart be healed and made whole? What if that caused you to see the world through a whole new, healthy lens you *didn't even know existed*? What if the glass on your world view lens is covered with smudges, *and you don't even realize it*? Maybe that's why the world looks so ugly to you?

What if going through the painful process of healing would

ultimately cause you to have *less pain*? What if you got new glasses that were cleaned and smudge-free so you could see the world around you the way that God wants you to see it? What if looking through a healthier, clean lens caused you to FINAL-LY spot your promised land and see the route to get there?

This has been my experience. The reward of going through healing is worth the difficulty of the process. Dealing with my "stuff" has led me to a fuller, happier, and a significantly more peaceful life. My healing process didn't eliminate difficult experiences from my life, but it made me more equipped to maintain my peace in the midst of them.

Healing also required me to delay my gratification. As an American, I'm not great at that. Americans tend to want *everything* and we want it *now*, don't we? We don't want a process; we want a magic pill. One thing is for sure: your free, full, happy peaceful life requires you to delay your gratification and go through *a process*. Will you do it?

Choosing to ignore hard things that have happened to us instead of processing through them is like saying, "I'll eat crackers and water for *every meal, every day,* as I progress toward death like all the other drones who are trying to avoid pain." This is the dreary, uncultivated option, but it is an option. Conversely, choosing to deal with our issues will be more onerous *at first,* but will lead to the satisfying life we were created for. Dealing with our wounds requires us to embark on a metaphorical fast, for a period. But then when you're done fasting, you'd get gourmet meals, cooked specifically to your taste.

Oh, and as a bonus, there are more jars of honey available to you when you choose healing. But first, you have to fast, and that means you're going to be hungry, and that will be hard. Would you be willing to let things get a little worse for a bit, so that they could ultimately end up so much better? Would you be willing to go off the beaten path to get the wild honey?

Oh, but let me guess. You don't think you've been through anything that would cause you to need healing? You don't think that you have issues you need to deal with? If you're thinking that, you might need healing more than most. Denial is uglier than Cinderella's step-sister. Don't take her in.

The reality is: life is hard and none of us walk through unscathed. Some of us have been wounded much more than others, but we've all been hurt. As we get hurt, we respond to that pain in a variety of ways. Sometimes we respond to pain in a way that limits our progress in life. It's wise to process our pain with someone else who is stable, knowledgeable, wise, and objective. Then we'll be more likely to develop a healthy perspective about what's happened to us and how we should respond to it. Having healthy responses will give us our best chance at living at peace with others and of prospering in life.

Your gourmet chef is waiting. But, first, the fast. Are you willing? It's worth it to fight for your promised land. It's flowing with milk and honey, or lattes and chocolate cookies, or margaritas and chips and salsa, or red wine and filets...or whatever would be in *your* promised land. I've gone through the process, and I'm currently standing in the most beautiful promised land with jars of honey waiting for me. Come with me. I'll show you why it's worth it.

Question: Would you be willing to take an honest look at your life and see if there are issues you need to address, and maybe even get the help of a counselor to deal with them? Be brave! You're worth it! Your promised land is waiting.

Endnotes:

1 Adkins, Adele. "Hello" Recorded 2015. XL.

2 Nin, Anaïs. US (French-born) Author and Diarist, 1903-1977. Accessed March 27, 2017. http://www.quotationspage.com/quote/38521.html.

3 Chesney, Kenny, Dean Dillon, and Scotty Emerick. "Boats." Recorded 2008. Blue Chair Records/BNA.

4 Hurston, Zora Neale. *Dust Tracks on a Road*. J. B. Lippincott, Inc., 1942.

5 Joel, Billy. "You're Only Human." Recorded 1985. Columbia Records.

CHAPTER 3

Baby Blue Caddy

Tell the devil I said, 'Hey' when you back to where you're from. [1]

"Do you have something specific that you'd like to talk about today?" my counselor asked.

"Actually, I do have something that I'd like to talk about. I want to talk about a 'butterfly feeling' in my stomach. It happens when I'd least expect it. I understand that happening in certain situations; but my stomach has butterflies at really odd moments when I'm not consciously aware of any stressors. I think something happens that triggers a stress reaction in me, but it's all happening at a subconscious level, so I don't know what it's connected to. I'd really like to figure out why that happens to me."

"Okay, let's ask Jesus about that." She began praying, "So, Jesus, is there anything that You'd like to tell Rachel about the 'butterfly feeling' in her stomach?"

As she prayed I immediately had a memory unfold. The memory is of something that happened to me when I was a little girl. In the memory, I see a boy to my left about three years old with a look of horror on his face. Over the boy's shoulder I see the springs of a garage door, toys, cubbies, and boxes. We're in a garage that's been converted into an in-home daycare. My vision pulls out a bit, and I can see he's one of many kids, and they're all standing in a circle. I am there, too.

There's an old woman with white curly hair wearing a red T-shirt with white writing on it, wire-rimmed glasses, and jeans that are pulled up so high they nearly reach her breasts. She's on the inside of the circle forcibly giving each child a cookie. With a bitter tone, she tells each little one, "Eat the cookie! Here, *eat this!*" Every child looks transfixed as he or she takes the cookie and begins to eat.

She gets around to me. I was so tiny. She gives me the cookie. I don't want to eat it, but that is *not* an option. I eat.

As I finish eating, the color drains from my little face. I start to cry and look around for someone to help me. There are other adults behind me, helpers of some sort, another woman and two men. I stumble towards them like I'm drunk, but the cranky old lady with the white curly hair intercepts me. She grabs me by the wrist and squeezes until it hurts. She pulls me towards the door that leads into the house as if she already knows what's going on with me. She drags me through a living room area to a bathroom and just before I reach the toilet, I begin throwing up. She's *furious* about that and begins swearing and raging about the mess I've made. I can only remotely make out what she's saying over the violent roars of my digestive system.

I interrupted my memory and told my counselor I was going to throw up. I looked for a garbage can. She calmed me and prayed, declaring that I will remember but will not relive, in Jesus's Name! A peace came over me.

Back in the memory I hear the old lady ranting about the mess I've made as I continue vomiting violently into the toilet. It's coming out my nose, and I feel like I can't breathe. I am panicking, and I lift my head as I get a break from the extraction of everything that had been in my belly. I see several people talking in the hallway about what to do with me because "It didn't work." I wonder, what didn't work? No time to contemplate that question as I'm back to vomiting. I'm so scared and *so* alone. None of the adults are tending to me. I can feel how angry they are at me. I stop throwing up. But soon I have diarrhea.

As I'm being shown this memory of myself, I begin to sense the other children who ate the cookies are in danger. Where are they? I consciously step out of the memory for a moment and begin to weep and weep and weep. "I know they're being hurt," I told my counselor.

"Who?" She asked.

"The other kids who are out in the garage eating cookies. Something really dark is happening to them" I sobbed. She shook her head yes. I saw the sadness in her face, too. As I recounted the events that took place there, I had a realization this is the preschool from hell, *literally*! This was a satanic coven claiming to be a preschool so they could train children in satanic rituals. That reality sunk in for the first time. I always knew how horrible that place was, but I never had a context for what had happened to me there. I thought that preschools in general were horrible places.

That day I begin to pray for the other children. Where are they now? What happened to them? I asked Jesus to heal all of them. I sobbed as I processed (now from an adult perspective) what happened there. I'd avoided thinking about that place my whole life until now. However, I couldn't avoid developing a cold sweat whenever I drove by preschools.

Because I'd never processed what happened to me there, I'd always held the belief that preschool is a dark, horrible place where parents selfishly send their kids. When we don't process things that happen to us as children, we can sometimes maintain a childish perspective of those events.

I go back into the memory and hear the sound of a bedroom door flying open and hitting the wall. Another woman with long, straight, gray hair who kind of resembles Meryl Streep comes storming out with fury on her face.

"What's the problem?" she yells. The lady with the short, white, curly hair answers with a trepidation that implies she failed. It's clear to me the lady with straight hair is smarter than the others. There's a hierarchy, and she's at the top. I'd come to learn that all cults and covens have a hierarchy system.

The curly-haired lady with glasses answers, "We did exactly what we were supposed to do. We gave her the same cookie we gave all the kids. She appears to be allergic or something. I don't know! I don't have time for this (expletive)!" She blurts out, throwing her hands up in bewilderment. They all then turn and stare at me as I sit on the toilet, trying to keep from falling in. I feel weak as I sit, letting the remains trickle out. I feel so stupid, so afraid, and *so* humiliated. I've messed everything up. They are highly annoyed with me. I didn't mean to do this, I didn't want to annoy them. I wanted to make them happy and be an obedient, good girl. I tried *so* hard. The little girl in me feels rejected.

My counselor broke in, and I'm "back" in the room with her. I needed a break from the anguish and despair this memory gives me. She asks Jesus to show me where *He* is in this memory and if there's anything He wants to say. At this point I switch from memory to a vision as Jesus answers my counselor's request.

As the vision began, I return to the position of throwing up. Only now, I see Jesus is kneeling next to me, rubbing my back, speaking to me, and comforting me. "It's okay. You're okay, Rach. Good job. Get out all that poison. You'll feel better once it's out," He gently whispers to me as I vomit. He's holding my hair back with one hand and rubbing my back with the other.

I hear the old ladies and at least one man talking about me again. As I listen to them, I am feeling rejected and despised. It's as if hatred is being sent at me like radio waves. My receiver picks up the signal, and I *feel* the hatred.

Then, out of nowhere, Jesus begins laughing hysterically. Little me is taken off guard and startled. My neck bends towards Him abruptly to see *why on earth* He's laughing! I'm stunned to see He's laughing at the other adults that are talking in the bathroom doorway. He laughs and laughs, and then catches His breath and says (pointing to my back), "*You messed with the wrong one!* She loves me, and you're going to be so sorry you messed with her." Then He throws His head back and cracks up exuberantly.

I stare at Him, jaw hanging open, as He's laughing. I *love* that He's laughing at them. Suddenly, through His laughter, their power over me evaporates. The truth about Jesus' superior authority goes deep into my spirit. As I watch Him laugh, I realize Jesus' power overrides their power. Just like that, in a microsecond their power that seemed so terrifying and strong seems like utter silliness compared to Jesus' authority.

Jesus then stops laughing and scans me, looking up and down. His assessment stops at my hair as He sees that it's gotten all messed up. He removes my little white hair clip, takes a little section of my hair and sweeps it over to the side, smoothing it out until it's just right. He puts the hair clip back in to hold my wave of hair in place, and says, "There." He then wipes my tears and cleans my face.

He cleans His hands, kneels back down to me, and puts His clean hand out to me, palm up. I look at His scarred hand and then back into His beautiful eyes. We smile at each other. I put my tiny hand in His. He goes from kneeling beside me to standing, to walking out of the bathroom, leading me behind Him. He's holding my hand tightly, and I know He's never going to let go.... *ever*. His grip on my hand is very firm, and perfectly tender all at the same time. He walks right through the center of these (literal) witches as they're talking about me. They're still talking, but they don't seem to notice we're leaving.

We get to the front door, and Jesus opens the door with one hand and escorts me out with the other. He appears to be keeping Himself between them and me, and He never lets go of my hand. He looks back at them, and His look condemns their actions. I think, *"I'd hate to be them!"* He closes the door, and I hear a sound like a metal bar falling and a big padlock clicking loudly into place.

Panic immediately creeps back into my little heart, so I glance back just to confirm they're not following us. Before I can get my head turned all the way around, Jesus captures my cheek in His hand. He softly turns my head back towards Him; we stop walking and face each other. He kneels in front of me and causes me to look deep into His beautiful eyes and as I do, I know *it's finished.*

My spirit receives a message from His Spirit: the power of this evil, the power of these people, the power of their activity in my life, *it's finished*. The fear, pain, and rejection associated with this memory-*finished!*" He communicates all this with a look in His eye. I nod my head as if to say, "I believe you." I suddenly realize that's why He said, "It is finished," as He was dying. Jesus came to destroy the works of the enemy, and that's exactly what this situation was. We smile again at one another. Jesus is so happy, really, joyful. I like Him *a lot!*

We continue walking, but now I have a spring in my step. I look down and see I'm wearing new clothes. I notice I'm wearing penny-loafers and white socks that are folded over and are lined with dainty lace. I'm wearing a flowing, navy blue skirt that hits just above my knee. I have on a simple white shirt with a folded down, lacy collar, and a short-sleeved, button-up sweater over it. The buttons are made of pearls like the gates of heaven. These clothes feel wholesome and sweet. I wonder if Jesus chose these new clothes because the preschool had always made me feel impure and defiled. After all, He is in the business of restoring dignity where it has been stolen.

Jesus and I are walking down the walkway towards the curb. He walks with strength, honor, and the ultimate power while simultaneously exuding sweetness, tenderness, and gentleness. He really is a marvelous mystery. I walk as if I really am a new creation, healing power filling my scrawny legs. My shoulders are back, chin is up, and my bluish/greenish eyes are sparkling. There's a peaceful, joyful assurance in each step.

Then, I freeze in my tracks as I see the coolest thing! Parked at the curb I see a ravishing, slate blue, 1964 Cadillac convertible. The chrome finishes are brilliant and shiny. The paint job is top of the line-stunning! Jesus leads me right up to it and opens the door for me. He leads me by my hand and helps me in. *This* is Jesus' car? I hop onto the pure white, leather seat that is just the right temperature on the back of my legs.

Jesus goes around and gets in. He starts the engine, and it had a purr that would make the most devoted, die-hard, car lover die. Jesus points to the glove box and says, "There's a jar of wild honey in there if you get hungry." I smile because I love wild honey. I kick off my penny loafers and put one foot on the dash, then cross my other one over the top. You might think that was rude of me, but Jesus is so cool. I can tell I'm welcomed to fully relax and just be myself in His presence, and I'm the kind that puts her feet on the dash. Jesus holds His hand out on the white leather bench seat, palm up again. I look down at the scarred hand He offers me and happily slide my tiny little hand into His once again. His fingers cover my entire hand. A feeling of security is transferred by osmosis.

We pull away from the curb; I don't look over at the house as we pull away, but up into the sun that's partially covered by a haze of clouds. I look at the sun while sitting next to The Son. Warmth floods my body and soul. As we drive a bit faster, a cool breeze lifts my hair and makes it fly, and I lean my head back on the white leather behind me. I close my eyes, and my hair blows backwards in the wind. I love it, the feeling of wind on my face. It feels like we're floating on clouds. I sneak a peek and realize *we are*! I look over at Jesus as if to say, *"This is so cool!"* Jesus smiles His eyes as if to say, *"I know, right?"* I smile from the inside out.

Jesus turns on the stereo, and I close my eyes and lean my head back again, listening to the lyrics:

There's a new wind blowing like I've never known.
I'm breathing deeper than I've ever done,
and it sure feels good to finally feel the way I do. [2]

I tap my feet to the music and think, "Ah, yes! Perfect!" Who knew Jesus was a Keith Urban fan? Coincidently enough, so am I.

Eyes to See That He Was Always There

The memory and vision end there, but the effects still impact me today. Just to clarify, I really was in that situation in the co-ven preschool, and the majority of what I just shared was a memory, not a vision. However, the effects of the traumatic memory were adjusted and healed when Jesus gave me a *vision* of Himself inserted into it.

Take a look at what the book of Revelation says about God in relation to time:

"'I am the Alpha and the Omega,' says the Lord God, 'who is
and who was and who is to come, the Almighty.'"
(Revelation 1:8, ESV)

Jesus is not bound by time. He can go back 35 years and insert Himself into something that happened to you and bring healing. He's actually not inserting Himself because He was always there. He just caused me to open my spiritual eyes and see Him there so He could heal me.

Have you ever had a vision? I hope you have. But whatever your experience, please don't dismiss my vision simply because you lack experience with them. Could you imagine if I said I did not believe racism or the Holocaust existed because I had never experienced either of them myself? Throughout the Bible people had visions.

That day in my counselor's office, Jesus gave me a vision and showed me He was with me in that tragedy. He was with me and was healing me from the effects it had on my life. If you struggle to believe visions could still be given, ask God to show you the truth. He's *all about* the truth! He invented it.

My truth is darker than most, not as dark as some. I dare not share my *whole* truth, because most people couldn't handle it and I don't want to talk about it. I hope your reality is tamer than mine. You don't have to be plunged to the heinous depths I have in order to understand pain and darkness. Maybe your parents divorced. Maybe you were bullied as a kid. Maybe you're overweight. Maybe you struggle with addiction. Maybe you've sinned in such a way that your haunted with regret. Regardless of where your pain comes from, know this: Jesus is in the middle of your pain with you, and He wants to heal you.

> *"The LORD is close to the brokenhearted and He saves those*
> *whose spirits have been crushed."*
> *(Psalm 34:18)*

Because of the depths of my pain, I've been comforted by Jesus Himself! Because my spirit has been crushed I've been saved by Him in multiple ways.

> *"Blessed are the poor in spirit for theirs is the Kingdom*
> *of Heaven. Blessed are those who mourn, for they shall be*
> *comforted." (Matthew 5:3-4)*

You know why Jesus was laughing so hard in my vision of us in the bathroom? His laughter came from a place of perfect knowledge. Jesus knew when someone is tortured by darkness, God will not only heal the trauma, but He will compensate us for it. He will bring justice to our scales. He *does not* make us as good as we were before the suffering; He makes us *better* than we would have been had we not been injured at all. He gives us extra gifts. He's literally near to us, and we see Him. We will be comforted by Jesus Himself.

I don't regret what I've been through. If I traded places with someone who had gone through less tribulation, that *might* mean I wouldn't have gotten to ride in Jesus's dope blue Caddy. That's not a trade worth making. Besides, I believe that the healed version of myself is better than the unwounded version would have been.

Question: Have you ever asked Jesus to show you where He was during a specific, difficult situation that you went through? Why not ask Him? Receiving His answer could be life-beginning for you.

Endnotes:

[1] Mars, Bruno, Philip Lawrence, Ari Levine, Brody Brown, Claude Kelly and Andrew Wyatt. "Grenade." Recorded 2010. Atlantic-Elektra.

[2] Urban, Keith, and John Shanks. "Somebody Like You." Recorded 2002. Capitol Records Nashville.

C H A P T E R 4

Break Time, Or Not

A man walks down the street.
He says, "Why am I soft in the middle now?
Why am I soft in the middle?
The rest of my life is so hard.
I need a photo opportunity.
I want a shot at redemption." [1]

In June 2014 I decided the cost of *not* blooming was worse than the cost of blooming. I wanted a shot at redemption, so I entered counseling to begin dealing with entirely unpleasant things like the preschool from hell. Blooming was hard and tiring. I've found that emotional pain often causes physical pain. So I was hurting, inside and out.

One afternoon my "soft in the middle" body, mind, soul, and spirit needed a break from healing! We lived in a neighborhood that had a community pool so, I took our four boys over there for some down time. Having "down time" with four boys in tow was not ideal, but you do what you've got to do.

There weren't many people at the pool that day, which was perfect because I didn't want anyone to bug me. My boys all hopped in the pool and started hitting a beach ball around. "One, two, three," they counted off, seeing how many hits they could get in before they missed. My youngest would always be the one that messed up, but the other three were so gracious with him. The way they gave him grace made my mama-bear heart happy. It was a rare and delightful moment where they were all four playing nicely together and even seemed to be enjoying each other.

I set up my waterproof, portable speaker and put on my favorite playlist which mostly consisted of Keith Urban, Jackson Browne, John Mayer, and a little Eagles thrown in here and there. I often use music to quiet my painful thoughts. I laid my towel on a lounge chair and faced the chair towards the sun to optimize the quality of my tan. Knowing how to optimize one's tan is a sure-fire sign you're a legitimate California girl.

I picked up my strongly brewed iced tea, sipped, and smiled. Ah, perfection! You know those times when your circumstances are just right and you get a little taste of heaven? I really took it in. Not one part of this bliss was lost on me. I felt so grateful for a precious moment of reprieve from my healing process.

After I'd been basking in the sunlit euphoria for approximately 3.5 Keith Urban songs, I heard the pool gate open. Without lifting my head to see who it was, I thought, "They better not mess *this* up!" I continued to keep my head down, as I didn't want my neck to have to work that hard; but then they came into my peripheral view. It was a mom pushing her daughter in a wheelchair. The daughter, whose undersized, mangled frame, appeared to be about 15 years old. I was a little surprised this mom would have her daughter sit out here in her wheelchair since it was over 100 degrees that day!

This duo had my attention. Without lifting my head, my eyes followed them while safely hiding behind my sunglasses. The mom rolled the girl around and parked her about 20 feet in front of me. I appreciated her parking there so I didn't have to lift my head, but could still spy.

From the moment they entered the pool area, the mom was talking to her daughter who appeared to be incapable of responding. It reminded me of when I'd talk to my infant sons while they'd stare at me in silence. The mom sat on a lounge chair and reached into her bag. She said to her daughter, "Are you excited? I am! It sure is hot today! The water is going to feel great!" I heard an unintelligible groan from the daughter. My spirit squirmed uncomfortably. The mom responded as if she could de-code the groan's true message the way that only a mom can. "Yes, it sure will feel great!"

The more I watched them, the more depressed I felt. This young girl was so very disfigured. Her quality of life, or lack thereof, made my lungs feel clogged. A lump formed in my throat as I considered what it'd be like to be them, *either* of them. Acid began burning my stomach, and bitterness circulated through my nervous system. I just wanted an hour or so to "check out" and *not* feel sad! Why did they have to come to the pool while I was there? They've messed up "my time." I'm embarrassed at my selfishness. But I didn't want to *feel* their issues, and I do tend to *feel* people's issues.

Then, my eyes opened a bit wider when I realized that the mom was blowing up floaties! Floaties? She was going to put this girl in the pool? I pictured this petite mom holding her disfigured, teenage daughter in the pool. I wondered how she'd get her out of her wheelchair and down into the pool with her. The mom was so petite. It seemed like this was going to be a struggle for them.

I watched as the mom wrestled the floaties up her daughter's maimed arm, all while talking to her so sweetly. The daughter continued with her unintelligible groans. The mom's tenderness was so sweet, yet this was entirely unpleasant to watch. What would it feel like to parent a child in this condition? What would it feel like to *be* a child in this condition? My heart ached. My resentment grew.

I didn't have long to consider their plight before the floaties were on, and the mom asked, "Are you ready?" No answer. She then put her hands on the wheelchair handles and started moving towards the edge of the pool. *Not towards the steps*, just towards the middle of the pool. Forget not wanting my neck to have to work, I sat straight up, neck lunging forward, and stared, wide-eyed! The mom got right up to the edge and started counting, one, two... The daughter's torso and head tipped towards the water, while something that resembled a smile was plastered across her face, like she was getting away with something. THEN, mustering all her physical strength, the mom starts to lift the back end of the wheelchair until her daughter *fell out of it!* She flopped into the pool with a loud splat in what would be coined a "10" in a belly flop contest.

I was *stunned!* My eyes were flashing all around the pool to see if anyone else just saw *that!* I looked at my boys, who were happily hitting their beach ball without a care in the world. They hadn't seen the girl. No one else around the pool would make eye contact with me so I could communicate with my eyes, "WHAT THE HECK JUST HAPPENED HERE, FOLKS?" This mom just dumped her *very* handicapped daughter into a pool with nothing but a couple of floaties for protection.

I stared at the pool's surface and held my breath. Then, up popped the girl's oversized head with her long molasses colored hair draped over, completely covering her face. She managed to push her nose and mouth through her hair and gasp for air. Then she squealed with delight. Her bent arms were going in and out of the water and were not in sync with one another. Her legs didn't appear to have any mobility. She flailed around like a mechanical duck that was malfunctioning. Then, without warning, I was overcome with emotion. Tears started rolling down my cheeks.

What on earth was I observing here? What becomes of a life like hers? Why was she alive? What was her purpose on this earth? She couldn't speak. She couldn't control her body. My body was heavy with sadness, as I grappled to understand exactly what it was that I was sensing.

But Then God

God spoke to my heart and said, "This girl's messy, awkward, graceless display in the pool feels familiar to you, doesn't it?" There were more tears, but from a different source of pain. He continued, "Right now your life feels like one gigantic cataclysmic tragedy, doesn't it?" I stared at the unwieldy body in the water and wanted to argue, but couldn't.

"Yes, I understand that's how *you're* feeling about your situation. But do you understand how *I* feel about your situation, about your life, your healing process?" God asked.

I contemplated the question and responded, "I guess I'd have to say no I don't. I mean not exactly. I know you love me, blah, blah, blah."

God continued, "Let the lens of your eye draw out a bit. Take your narrow focus off what's happening in the pool, and look at what's happening next to it."

My eyes shifted poolside where I saw the girl's mom, whom I'd assumed would probably be crying too. Not only was she *NOT* crying, she was glowing, *beaming* with pride! Her mouth was open in wonder as her eyes were locked in on her flailing daughter. Her eyes were not filled with tears, but were dancing with elation! Her laughter seemed to spring out of a deep well of joy as she said over and over and over, "Look at you! Look at you! Look at you! *Aren't you something*! I'm so proud of you. Wait till daddy sees this! Wow! You're doing so well! Good job!" She said this between pure, unadulterated bursts of laughter.

She had her iPhone out, filming *every* second of what felt like a catastrophe. She followed her daughter closely, as if she didn't want to miss a single thing. Then, I realized it's not that she doesn't want to miss a thing. She's filming this as if she'd want to watch this *again*! My tears were squirting out as my chest and my chin quivered. I pushed my sunglasses up and turned away from the pool, towards God's presence within me. What is *this that I'm feeling*?" I began to sense that deep within me, wounds were being treated and bandaged up, but I didn't really understand how or why.

Then, as only God can, He spoke to my spirit in a way that breeds life. He spoke in a way that was three dimensional. I found it hard to translate what God said because sometimes He speaks in a way that supersedes words and cognitive reasoning. He said something like, "You feel like your life is such a disaster right now, a tragic mess. You feel like an awkward, flailing, handicapped girl, and like that's all you'll ever be. When you look in the mirror you see a girl that's mangled beyond repair, and you for sure think that's how others see you. In fact, many others do judge you and see you that way. You're wondering why you're even alive and what purpose your life could serve when it's been so mangled. Don't you?"

My spirit answers Him without words as I release soft sobs poolside.

He continued, "But that's not at all how I see you. I'm watching you go through this healing process, and I'm beaming with pride. I'm cheering for you. I'm talking to you, even when you can't or won't respond. I see your life, with all its deformities, missteps, and tribulations. I'm not in denial about the dark reality. I'm not a human that I would *ever* turn away from the truth or try to cover it up. I'm at your counseling appointments, in your closet floor as you lament, and in your bed as you try to sleep away the pain. I watch you doing the hard work of healing and say, "Look at you! Look at you! Look-at-you! Aren't you *something*?! I'm so proud of you! Wait till the angels see this! Wow! You're doing so well! Good job!"

He went on, "Precious, Rachel, please remember that one of my favorite things to do for those who love Me is to take their handicapped, mangled, awkward, sick, malfunctioning lives, and turn them into Olympic swimming, gold-medal winners. I told you about this in Romans 8:28 and 1 Corinthians 2:9. When I see you and what you're going through, I see an Olympic Medal Winner in training, and it's beautiful. I see redemption in process. The redemptive process is messy at times, but beautiful, *so very beautiful.*"

God's Repayment Plan

God continued to download a concept into my spirit that day that has become very important to me. He began to teach me that those of us who have been hurt, rejected, abused, betrayed, abandoned, maligned, ridiculed, stolen from, tortured, or traumatized are often the ones that have the greatest gifts inside of us. It is that very potential, that gift God has put in us, that X-factor, that causes evil to go after us so diligently. Darkness is attempting to loot our souls and steal our treasures. More specifically, when Satan saw that our God-given destiny was to be a highly effective world changer, he set out to harm us until we gave up. Satan aspires to keep us from becoming whatever God intends for us to become.

There are some problems with Satan's plans to hinder us though. *When we maintain a heart that is open to God, in spite of how we've been hurt, we are then given opportunities to receive unimaginably greater gifts, or compensations, to offset Satan's activity in our lives.* That's justice. That's God's way. He loves justice and mercy and humility, and He wants us to love those things, too. Why do you think Jesus said that He came to destroy the works of the evil one? When the evil one attacks us, Jesus gives us double for our trouble (*at least double, usually more)!* God Himself set up a system for His people that shows His heart towards these types of issues. When a thief steals, he must pay back more than what he stole.

Take a look at that concept in these scriptures:

> *"Whoever steals an ox or a sheep and slaughters it or sells it must pay back five head of cattle for the ox and four sheep for the sheep."*
> *(Exodus 22:1)*

"And we know that in all things God works for the good of those who love him, who have been called according to his purpose."
(Romans 8:28)

"All things" means, ALL THINGS, even the really bad things.

"Anyone who steals must certainly make restitution, but if they have nothing, they must be sold to pay for their theft. If the stolen animal is found alive in their possession — whether ox or donkey or sheep — they must pay back double."
(Exodus 22:3-4)

"If anyone grazes their livestock in a field or vineyard and lets them stray and they graze in someone else's field, the offender must make restitution from the best of their own field or vineyard."
(Exodus 22:5)

"If anyone gives a neighbor silver or goods for safekeeping and they are stolen from the neighbor's house, the thief, if caught, must pay back double."
(Exodus 22:7)

I wonder if His compensation plan is part of what Jesus was showing us in these Beatitudes as well:

"Blessed are the poor in spirit,
for theirs is the kingdom of heaven.
"Blessed are those who mourn,
for they will be comforted.
"Blessed are the meek,
for they will inherit the earth.
"Blessed are those who hunger and thirst for righteousness,
for they will be filled.
"Blessed are the merciful,
for they will be shown mercy.
"Blessed are the pure in heart,
for they will see God.
"Blessed are the peacemakers,

for they will be called children of God.
"Blessed are those who are persecuted because of righteousness,
for theirs is the kingdom of heaven.
"Blessed are you when people insult you, persecute you and
falsely say all kinds of evil against you because of me.
"Rejoice and be glad, because great is your reward in heaven, for
in the same way they persecuted the prophets who were before
you."
(Matthew 5:3-12)

And think about this promise…

"However, as it is written: 'What no eye has seen, what no ear
has heard, and what no human mind has conceived' — the things
God has prepared for those who love Him — "
(1 Corinthians 2:9)

"For those who love Him"… The principle in Scripture is this: God's way is not to give someone back what was taken from him. He gives him back *more or better* than what was taken. When Satan harms us (usually by way of another person), then God requires a double portion to be given to us in return. So if Satan steals $100 from us, we don't just get $100 back; we get $200 *or more*. I've seen this in my own life over and over. This concept was written into God's law and is throughout Scripture.

Prerequisites

There are prerequisites for us receiving from God in this way. We are not blessed because we've been hurt. We are blessed because God redeems our pain in a way that makes the pain worth it. We're also blessed because of the reason Satan went after us to begin with. He tried to wound us because of the extraordinary riches God had put in us upon our creation.

So how can we attain God's reimbursement for our troubles?

Notice that 1 Corinthians 2:9 and Romans 8:28 are written for those of us who *love God.* So the first prerequisite for receiving that double portion compensation for our pain is that we need to love God. That means we can't blame God for our pain. We can't attribute the works of the enemy to God. How do we love God? To know God is to love God. The more we know Him, the more we will love Him. A good starting place for getting to know Him is to study His Word.

The second prerequisite is we must bring our wounds to God and *ask* Him for justice. Sometimes we have not because we ask not.

> *"Whatever it is that you need or want, ask God for it."*
> *(James 4:3)*

And sometimes we *do have,* but we don't see that we have because our eyes are fixated on the wrong things or they're closed all together.

Which brings me to the third prerequisite. We have to get our spiritual eyes and vision fixed. God may have been giving us opportunities to receive blessings and compensations from Him, but our eyes were so messed up we were blinded to the opportunities. Our world view lens may have too many smudges on it. We get our spiritual vision fixed when we go through a healing process and deal with our wounds. Then, we are more likely to see the world in a healthy way. We're also more likely to recognize God's activity in our lives.

I would like to present to you a possibility I hope you'll sincerely consider: If you've been hurt in your life, it's because there's a treasure inside of you. There is a God, and there really is an enemy of God. Satan hates everything good. He hates everything that's pure. He hates bright lights, so when he saw the magnitude of the treasure God had given you, he set out to steal it or at least defile it. His hope was if he wounded you enough, you were never going to put your floaties on and get in the pool.

In many cases, he's been right. There are many people who don't want to deal with the wounds of their past. They just try to stuff it down and forget about it. Many think there's nobility in moving on, or just "getting over it." It almost feels like that's a subtle, subconscious, religious message that many perceive. I'd like to suggest that if we "just move on" and don't deal with our wound, it's left to fester and bubble up and continue to sabotage our lives.

Another tactic the enemy employs is to convince you that you don't need healing. You're fine. You don't have anything to deal with. Just move on. Stay busy. Have a drink. Hop online. Don't allow yourself to think *too much*. Just numb that pain a little, you'll be fine. Warning: his voice can sound suspiciously similar to your own. Maybe as you've been reading this you've already thought, "Well, I don't have anything that needs healing." I thought that too. I was wrong. We might want to consider the fact that none of us gets out of this life unscathed. Chances are good we have some things and if we'd deal with them, we could experience a new-found freedom.

We can't let Satan win because he bet *against us*! He loves Las Vegas! He's placed bets against your ever finding and living in your promised land, fulfilling the purposes for which you were created. His goal is to keep you on the path of the wounded masses so you never discover how scrumptious the taste of wild honey is.

Get in that wheelchair, put on those floaties, tip forward, flop and swim. You've got to start somewhere. Deep within you there is a well-preserved treasure that God has kept safe. You've just got to let Him treat the wounds that have come through the years. As you do, your eyes will be fixed, and I promise you'll be amazed at what you'll see. He'll heal each wound, one by one; and as He does, you'll make your way back to that pure-hearted person that's been there all along. Then, before you know it, you won't even need floaties anymore. Little by little, day by day, your arms won't be bent anymore. Your legs won't be paralyzed. You'll swim like a pro, and the whole process will have been worth it!

Figuring Out What's at the Root

Wounds, betrayals, our parents' divorce, bitterness, failed businesses, our spouse leaving us, unhealthy sexual situations, our child turning on us, people from our church rejecting us, and all other issues we haven't dealt with, can prevent us from entering our "promised land." They'll keep us from living in the center of God's will and living to our highest potential. There's more for you, sweet one! This *isn't* as good as it gets! Ever asked yourself, "Is this it? Is this all there is to life?" I certainly asked that before my healing process! And the answer is: Yes, there IS more than *this*!

Ask God this question: "What issues of the heart do I need to deal with so I can be all You created me to be?" Then, take time to listen. He might answer you immediately, or you might have the answer revealed to you over some time.

If you feel like you struggle to hear an answer, this might help: look at what kinds of things make you angry. Ask yourself: what kind of issues or subjects cause me to try to distract myself so I don't have to think about or deal with them? Try to look at knee-jerk reactions you have. Look at the dreams you have at night.

62

Look at what makes you afraid. What makes you feel vulnerable? Ask yourself: in what area of my life do I feel like a victim? As you think over your life, look for patterns. Do you have any issues or specific kinds of wounds that seem to repeat themselves in your life?

Asking yourself and God these questions will help you figure out what might need healing in your life. Going to a good counselor can also help you figure out areas that need healing. You have a promised land that is waiting, and it's going to be good! It's going to be worth getting to the bottom of your heart issues, dealing with them, and being healed. You were created for greatness, sweet thing. You are a bright light, and this hurting world desperately needs you to shine, fulfilling your highest potential. You have something specific you can contribute to the world around you. Be brave. Ask God, and yourself, those questions. I'm excited for you! Your future is bright! The world is waiting.

Endnote:

1 Simon, Paul. "You Can Call Me Al." Recorded 1986. Warner Bros.

CHAPTER 5

Childhood Comes For Me At Night

The booming drum sound in my brain is so loud I'm unable to make out their words. There's wicked laughter I *am* able to hear, but only as if through a muffled filter. My breath, quick. My palms, moist. In fact, my whole body is wet with the kind of perspiration that terror births. I'm running, but I can feel them *right* behind me. I dare not bend my neck back to check; there's no time for that. I reach the door. I grab the handle. I open my mouth to release an agonizing scream for help, but nothing comes out. My voice fails me. Evil grabs the collar of my shirt and drags me back to the "situation." I close my eyes. Tears still manage to force their way out. I beg. My begging, unsuccessful. The memory goes black.

I awaken to my body springing itself into an upright position in my bed. I'm gasping for air, and that same heart, albeit a little older, is beating painfully loud again. Its rhythm is intense, like the sound of a perfectly timed drum major leading an award-winning marching band. BOOM, BOOM, BOOM, BOOM.

Oh, thank God it was only a reenactment, only a "remembering dream." Oh, thank God I'm bigger. I'm stronger. I can fight meaner and run faster. My voice is louder now. They wouldn't keep me in that dark situation *now*. Oh, thank God. I'm okay. Everything's going to be OKAY, I hope. *I pray.* The drum major slows his beat to a steady boom....boom....boom...

Why do I keep having these dreams? They barge in at night like an annoying neighbor that drops by at the most inconvenient times. During the day I forget very well, but not at night. The work of forgetting is tiring. Not to mention that forgetting software takes up a lot of space on one's mental hard drive. But, the sadness that remembering brings is worse, so I persist in the endeavor. I've been able to forget the worst. My mind knows that it's only allowed to go so far, and then it's been given strict orders to cease and desist remembering anything *too* painful. I find my mind to be obedient with these orders, *except* when I sleep.

Time to get ready for the day. Wipe away the sweat and the tears. Breathe deep. Smile and protect the others from being sad. After all, there's no use in us *all* being sad...and...scared... and tormented. I'll take one for the team. I'll just borrow some of their happiness like any well-performing co-dependent child would. They seem to be so unaware of the darkness, and I want to protect their naivety. It's no surprise they manage to stay happy. It seems as though ignorance really is bliss for them. So darkness stays tucked away in its favorite, secret hiding spot. Only a selfish brat would burden others with this kind of darkness, and I'm not a brat. I'm a sweet girl, *or at least I want to be one so badly.*

I think about my parents and how much I love them. I consid-

er telling them, but then quickly conclude I cannot. I do everything I can to keep them from experiencing pain. I sense they
can't handle it. I, on the other hand, *can* handle it. I'm a big girl,
and I can handle this all by myself. I just need to get over the
"situations." After all, I'm not little anymore; I'm six years old.

Wake Up Already!

Well these days I wish I was six again.
Oh make me a red cape.
I want to be Superman. [2]

I look down from the top bunk in our shared, apartment bedroom to see if my little brother is awake. He's not. I'm glad.
Then, I'll get dad's attention all to myself. I put my hands in between the mattress and the edge of my bunk and then flip my
body over in a summersault motion and land with my feet on
the ground. I head to the door, quietly closing it so that Ryan
doesn't wake.

I tip-toe out to the living room, and I find dad, who has fall-
en back asleep on the couch. He's on his tummy with his hand
folded up under his cheek. He looks like a crippled boy I once
saw who had his hand permanently bent at the elbow and wrist
and its pressed against his cheek. I stare at him for several seconds hoping my fixed gaze will wake him. Most nights dad can't
sleep, so he takes catnaps as the rest of the world is rising from
their slumber. My peering intensely doesn't wake him, so I intentionally make noise so I'll accidentally wake him.

"Good morning, bluebird." He says in a groggy morning voice.

With a mischievous grin inside I say, "Oh, sorry, did I wake
you?" and I prance over and climb onto his back and lay down on
it. "Will you make waffles?" I ask.

He pauses to consider something. I'm not sure what, but I do know the pause is only a façade because he'll say "yes."

He responds, "I suppose so."

See? I told you he'd say yes. He gets up and makes waffles for me, and I go on adoring him as I wish all six-year old girls could adore their dads. I think he's perfect, and I so want him to think I'm, well, at least good. I can tell he does. The fear and shame my nightmare re-enactment gave me has quickly evaporated, and all is well, other than that constant gnawing, burning ball of fire in my belly that tells me something horrible might happen at any given second. Terror is like a baby from hell that is stuck in the birth canal. Other than *that*, in this moment, all is well.

I talk dad's head off as he tiredly prepares my breakfast. I eat my waffles and head in to shower for school. As I shower I feel cornered by darkness again. Like it was just waiting to get me alone where I had no one to protect or distract me. My mind starts racing, and on cue, the drum major lifts his hands and prepares to lead the band again. BOOM, BOOM, BOOM. The waffles are creeping up my digestive track. I swallow hard and try to think about something else. I am absolutely paranoid about throwing up, so I distract myself with the soap. I love the smell of Coast soap. Mmmm, I taste it. Ooh, ugh, yuck. Note to self: it smells a lot better than it tastes.

I need to fully make the transition from the scared-out-of-her-ever-loving-mind-girl to the strong one before I exit the shower. The shower feels like my dressing room. I step in as Clark Kent, make some subconscious, mental adjustments and step out as Superman. Nearly every superhero has a tragic past, don't they? I wonder if it's the very nature of our tragedies that makes us into something gallant and kind of superhuman. At six-years old I didn't feel heroic. I felt terrified, but I could pretend otherwise quite effectively. And just like that-the art of compartmentalizing is being mastered.

I'll get really good at that, thinking about something else to avoid pain. So good, in fact, I'll *almost* forget it all together. I'd better get used to that heart pounding, stomach turning, palms sweating, nausea, fear thing too because as it turns out there'll be a lot more of that in my future. There will also be a lot more dreams, both good and bad. I didn't know it then, but dreams would end up becoming a huge part of my human experience, as would waffles.

So, while I'd attended the preschool from hell and by this point had been molested by a next-door neighbor, I also had a lot of good in my life. My dad gave me such sweet gifts that few fathers give their children. Again, the yin and yang in my life were extreme. While my dad couldn't spoil me with material things, he spoiled me with emotional blessings. He made me feel like I could do anything, and I usually believed him. I wish every dad would do that for their children.

I always felt that there was absolutely nothing I could do to make him stop loving me. My dad is the poster child for unconditional love. When I was with my dad, I felt like I was treasured, and like I was invincible. My sweet dad also made me waffles all the time, just about anytime I asked. Once when we were out of milk and our car was broken down, he rode my banana seat, lavender, little girl's bike with the daisy covered basket on the front to the store to get more. He was fun. He made our lives fun. So, while there were many unfortunate things I experienced, there were even more fortunate things. I once heard a girl certain of her father's love was destined for greatness. I'd hoped that was true because I was certain.

While a mother's love is clearly important in the life of a child, there's just something particularly powerful about having a godly, loving, esteeming, supportive father. As a mother myself I wish that I believed my love and support were just as important as my husband's, but in my gut I don't believe that. I think that a father's role is *extremely* important in a child's development or lack thereof. The most insecure people I know aren't confident of their father's love.

If you didn't have your father's love and support, there's healing for you! I pray that God will show you the love of a father in some other way. Lacking your father's love is something that can be healed and overcome. If your father was not there for you in the ways that you needed him to be, please know that was because of his issues and his free-will. It wasn't a reflection of you or your worth. If you're not certain of your father's love, there's a good chance that's affecting your ability to have relationship with God. I'd encourage you to seek healing for that wound.

Surprise, They're Actually Gifts!

In my healing process, I discovered those abominations I worked so hard to forget were actually gifts. They were disguised though. At first glance they looked like cruel and unusual punishments. That's why it took me 38 years to see them as gifts. As each wound was redeemed, I was able to see their gift-like nature. My wounds became gifts because of God's repayment plan that I discussed in chapter 4.

Did you ever say, "Life's not fair!" when you were a kid? I said that a lot, and we were right. Life is not fair! Many kids didn't have the kinds of trauma and the emotional issues that ensue the way I had. Most probably didn't have the kinds of tormenting nightmares I had. Most didn't go to the preschool from hell.

There's a whole lot of girls that weren't molested by their neighbor. That's not fair.

However, many kids also didn't know the love of a gentle, fun, godly, esteeming dad the way I did. It's remarkable to me how far the love of a father can take a girl. My dad's love covered a multitude of sins in my life. There was so much that was wrong, but because of my dad's unconditional love for me, I was often pretty confident. I think the love my dad showed me is a main reason why the abominations that happened in my life didn't destroy me.

As an adult I'd come to learn that my dad was battling his own demons, nightmares, and torment. I'd discover that while he was dishing out all that unconditional love, he was battling addiction and extreme emotional pain from his own childhood trauma. I was nearly 30 years old before I learned these things about my dad, and it made me love him even more. I realized that all those years of him smiling every time I walked into a room, all those times he would reach out and grab me as I walked by just to hug me and tell me how wonderful I was, those were years that he was barely surviving. When I was 30 years old and he was 52, he entered his own counseling/recovery process. He faced his demons and overcame them. My dad was wonderful when I was growing up, but now I get to enjoy the redeemed version of him, and he's even better.

Fathers, don't underestimate how powerful your love, affirmation, and attention are in the life of your children. If you weren't the kind of father you wanted to be and your kids are grown, you can still express your love and approval of them now. Give them your approval. TELL them some kind of affirming, approving message. Even after years of doing it wrong, you can change.

Just Try To Look Normal

So after waffles and showering, I finished getting dressed in my hand-me-down clothes and off to school I rode on my hand-me-down bike. I can't imagine letting a six-year-old ride her bike to school alone in today's world, but in 1982 there I went. As I rode I would mentally prepare myself to try to appear normal. I went through my checklist of things that the 'normal' kids did so that I could accurately mimic them. I may not *be* normal, but I was sure going to *look* normal. It was so much work to appear normal when from the tiniest of ages I had been catapulted from the normal kids to the traumatized ones. Hard work builds character though, right? If that were true, I was lucky to have so much work to do.

As lucky as I was, I honed my acting skills to trick as many people as possible into thinking that I was just a normal kid. I'd later learn we lucky ones should just let ourselves be lucky without shame. But when you're six, you don't understand about these things. So, I masked my true identity and acted as if I had no luck at all. Instead, I acted like I was a black belt in karate that was a huge Michael Jackson fan.

Satan will often make us feel like we are weird in a world full of normals, but that is a lie. We're all weird, just to differing degrees. I was so weird, but so were you. Actually, I still am weird. Healing didn't take my weirdness go away. You might not have been quite as weird as me, but you were weird! You probably talk to yourself, don't you? Yeah, see, that's weird. That's OKAY though. Who gets to define normal and weird anyway? Being normal and being weird are such relative terms. We're all weird and we're all normal.

Today, ask God to shine light on any area of your life where you've believed the lie that you're too weird to be acceptable to a community of people. Have you ever felt that if people knew the real you, you wouldn't have any friends? I'd like to be honest with you: there will be some people who will not accept the real you. That's sad, but true. However, once the real you emerges, your particular tribe will come out of nowhere and will embrace you wholeheartedly. Your *true* friends will make a circle around you and say, "We see you, *the real you*, and we approve." That beautiful circle of friends doesn't circle around you and give you that message until the real you reveals itself.

If you continue to hide your true identity you'll continue to have disingenuous friendships. The people you think are your friends are not necessarily your friends. They're friends to whom you're presenting yourself to be, not with *you*. When you stop trying to act like you're "normal", and get healing and reveal the real you, a beautiful thing transpires. Your friendships become authentic. The people who love you, the real you, stick around and embrace you more than ever. I found that as I revealed the real me, a whole host of new friends were drawn to me, too. The people who were drawn were wonderful, authentic people who let me see the real them in exchange for my willingness to do the same. The depth of relationship that can transpire in this kind of open, honest environment is one of the most rewarding human experiences.

You are *not alone* in your weirdness, pain, and your shame. You are *not* the only one that feels that way. Any time we believe "no one would understand," "I'm so weird," or "I can't tell anyone because they're all so normal and I'm not," we are believing lies. Anytime we keep these kinds of secrets in our souls, we maintain a playground for Satan. He loves secrets so he tries to intimidate us into thinking that we're misunderstood misfits that belong on the island of misfit toys. Truth:

We're all misfits and the island where we belong is beautiful.

Question to ask yourself: Is there anything I've been through in my life that makes me feel like "I'm the only one" or like "no one would understand"? If so, that's probably something that is embodying a lie. Ask God to show you if you need to talk to someone about it.

Endnote:

1 Mayer, John. "83." Recorded 2003. Columbia, Aware, SMV Enterprises.

CHAPTER 6

Every Little Part Of Me Is Going To Be OK

Well, she was precious like a flower
She grew wild, wild but innocent
A perfect prayer in a desperate hour
She was everything beautiful and different
Stupid boy, you can't fence that in
Stupid boy, it's like holding back the wind
She laid her heart and soul right in your hands
And you stole her every dream and you crushed her plans
She never even knew she had a choice and that's what happens
When the only voice she hears is telling her she can't
Stupid boy, stupid boy
So what made you think you could take a life
And just push it push it around
I guess to build yourself up so high
You had to take her and break her down
She laid her heart and soul right in your hands
And you stole her every dream and you crushed her plans
She never even knew she had a choice and that's what happens
When the only voice she hears is telling her she can't
You stupid boy

Oh, you always had to be right but now you've lost
The only thing that ever made you feel alive
Well, she laid her heart and soul right in your hands
And you stole her every dream and you crushed her plans
Yes, you did
She never even knew she had a choice and that's what happens
When the only voice she hears is telling her she can't...
It took awhile for her to figure out she could run
But when she did, she was long gone, long gone
Ah, she's gone, she's long gone.
Yes, she's gone [1]

Happy Birthday, Rach!

By the time that I turned four-years-old, I had experienced the kind of trauma that horror films are made of, the kind that causes one to dissociate. But, don't feel sorry for me. Remember Jesus' slate blue Cadillac? I'll explain more about the term 'dissociate' later. By the time I was six, a neighbor had molested me. I was also six years old when I met a pastor that would play a huge role in my life. When I was six, I had one of my favorite teachers of all time, Mrs. Jones. She was that beautiful African-American woman who taught me about the civil rights movement and about standing up for the "least among us." I adored her!

Mrs. Jones' influence called out the justice-seeker in me. Her influence on my desire to see justice remains strong to this day. Remember how I said that I wore a Michael Jackson pin for one of my teachers? It was for the oh-so-wonderful Mrs. Jones. I sure hope that pin made her happy the way being in her class made me happy!

When I was six and in the middle of first grade, my family moved from one city to another and that's when Mrs. Jones became my teacher. When I was six, I also had a crush on boy named David. He had a fine-looking bowl-cut hairdo that framed his face and highlighted his lengthy eyelashes beautifully. Six is also the number most people associate with Satan.

The pastor I met when I was six became a close family friend. He was at our house a lot, as if he were part of the family. He'd often take my brother and me out to do fun things like play miniature golf or go to the movies. So it was not a big surprise when he asked my parents if he could take me out on "a date" for my tenth birthday. He said he wanted to take me out for my first date ever. He wanted to do something extra special for me since I would only turn ten once. Boy, did he!

Destitution marred our family, so his gifts were welcomed and very appreciated! As my entry into double digits approached, so did he. He asked my parents if he could take me to a fancy restaurant to celebrate, just him and me. My parents agreed. I was a bit nervous, but excited at the same time. I was excited because I would dress up and go to a fancy restaurant! I was nervous because, well, I didn't know why. At that point, I'd never heard of *discernment*.

My birthday arrived and again, so did he. He came on the scene in a three-piece, grey suit and a white Chevy Blazer. I was in my favorite denim-colored dress with the lacy trim. My hair was curled and I wore my white tights with shiny, black patent leather shoes. It all felt so special. *I* felt so special.

We posed for some pictures the way you do before going to the prom, then left to go to dinner. I felt so jittery and uncomfortable even though I'd spent hours upon hours with this man before that night. Why was I so nervous? I felt guilty for feeling uncomfortable; after all, he was being generous and doing something nice for me.

At dinner we talked about what seemed to be adult-like things.
I liked that! He told me at times he forgot I was even a kid because I was so mature. That compliment made me straighten my
posture and hold my head high with pride. "I'm so mature," I
thought, as I drank my Shirley Temples like they were going out
of style, fishing every Maraschino cherry out of the ice and eating them just to put my maturity on display. That was before the
day of free refills, but I was told I could have as many as I wanted, and so I did. For dinner I ordered shrimp scampi, and it was
delicious. I was not a cheap date.

After dinner it felt like the tables turned. The pastor fidget-
ed and shifted in his seat like he was the nervous one now. He
looked around the restaurant, and then down at his plate, and
then finally up at me. He said, "I had a very special reason why
I wanted to take you on this date for your birthday." He paused
and looked deep into my eyes with a soul-penetrating stare, as if
he was trying to determine what my response would be to something he was going to say.

My stomach did a quick back flip and my ears focused sharp-
ly to catch his next words. He continued, "The reason I took you
out tonight is...you know you're *very* special to me, don't you?
You're *very* special to me! I think you and I make a good team.
We're good together. I think we are going to get married one
day, and when we do you'll get to say, 'My husband took me on
my first date ever!' Wouldn't that be neat?"

I began to fold and re-fold my napkin and shift my white
tights around under the table. Sweat started filling my pores. My
scrawny 10-year-old body felt heavy and confused sitting in that
fancy, leather booth. His 26-year-old one looked stimulated.

I looked at his brown hair that looked like a wig made of small
piles of cat poop. Then my eyes shot down to his mustache. As

hot as Magnum PI was at the time, it wasn't my thing. Facial hair? I didn't even shave my legs yet! To me, he was a surrogate uncle, like a second father. I'd never dreamed of my marrying my uncle or dad. I dreamed of marrying Kevin Bacon from "Footloose" or maybe Alex P. Keaton from "Family Ties." But this guy, never.

I nervously laughed at his words. I reached down and fiddled with the buckles on my patent leather shoes as if fixing them became a four-alarm emergency. I unlatched the patent leather strap and then re-buckled it. There was nothing left to do, so I looked up into his muddy eyes. They stared at me with a serious, inquisitive tone. His elbows were on the table, which grandma had always said was improper. Shame on him! This was a nice restaurant, he should have known better.

I made a joke so *he would think I thought* he was joking. His silence spoke volumes. He wasn't joking at all, and he was looking at me with lust. My heart sank into my stomach and now they were both doing back flips. He was ruining what had been such an exciting night. My muscles began to ache with feelings of homesickness and deep, betraying sadness. I just wanted to go home. I wanted my mom. He wanted to order dessert and keep this romantic conversation going.

Let "Happy Agreeable" Deal With It

My dissociation skills kicked in at that point. I unknowingly put on the face of the "happy, agreeable girl" that could do *anything* required of her to survive. We traumatized ones will sometimes create these elaborate escape routes for our minds. Well, we don't create them. God creates them for us. We use these escape routes in times when reality crosses that indelible line between acceptably difficult and insanely cruel.

Once that line was crossed, my mind would switch from "me" to the part of me that handled traumatic events. I would call this "losing time," but the technical term for it is "dissociation." Dissociation can feel like you're floating out of your body and someone else comes in to man it for you. It can feel like a memory suddenly goes completely black and then picks back up later. Your conscious mind drifts from reality to a happier place. I'd have a segment of time I just couldn't remember, like a blackout, so to speak. Even what I did remember I didn't tell.

During the ride home this man coached me on what I could and could not share with my parents as he reached over and put his hand on my leg. He helped me to "get in their heads" and explained they wouldn't understand how special and *unique* our relationship was, so I shouldn't tell them anything about it.

I know, it's all so predictable, isn't it? The close family friend gets in good with the family who's living in poverty and starts grooming the young daughter. Then, at just the right moment when the grooming and earned trust seem to be far enough along, the sexual advances begin. My sad and unfortunate situation bore all the obvious markings of an inappropriate situation, yet it went undetected by those who could have done something about it, including people in our church who I'd later learn "could tell something wasn't right."

The 2015 film *Spotlight* [2] (which won the Academy Award for Best Picture along with Best Original Screenplay) did a fantastic job of showing how people in positions of spiritual authority can use their power to prey on the most vulnerable among us. They are often trusted without question which gives them unprecedented access. Obviously, there are some wonderful people in positions of spiritual authority, but it's wise to be aware that *some* people sought out those positions because it would give them a means of entry into the lives of those they intended to harm and take advantage of.

As an adult when I finally told on this man, there were quite a few people who said they sensed my relationship with this man was inappropriate. I'm grieved when people say this to me because had they spoken up, maybe I could've been spared so much heartache. Silently they stood by speculating, gossiping, and judging our family in the privacy of their homes as I went on being abused by this pastor. Doesn't that remind you of the quote:

> *"The only thing necessary for the triumph of evil*
> *is that good men do nothing."* [3]

My life demonstrates the validity of this quote. Good people did nothing, and evil triumphed for too many years. Let's not be spectators and gossipers when something doesn't seem right. At the very least, pray! Pray any darkness that's occurring will be exposed! If led, do something more than pray.

Have you ever been betrayed by someone you thought you could trust? Ever been hurt by someone who should have been safe? Anyone ever walked out of your life when he promised to stay forever? Ever gone unprotected by someone whose main job description included protecting you? Has someone who said he was an ambassador from heaven ever taken you through hell? Ever had someone you thought was a fellow sheep suddenly act like a wolf?

I believe even if our stories are different, we can understand each other's pain on some level. I think that's because pain understands pain, even if the source of the pain is different. Does that comfort you? It does me. It comforts me to know if you have experienced deep levels of sadness, rejection, betrayal or pain, then in some way we can relate to one another. We can have a fellowship in a place where we're understood. I can sympathize with your heartbreak, and you mine. We're not totally alone in it. Even if we're on different levels of the pain spectrum, we can extend compassion. Perhaps it's true, misery does love company.

I obeyed and feared this pastor, and in a lot of ways was controlled by him for years. I didn't tell my parents the things he said and did to me. Some of what he did to me I completely blocked out from my conscious brain for a period of time. What he did with me was so traumatic my mind used dissociation to cope with the trauma.

What is Dissociation?

Dissociation is something that happens *involuntarily* when extreme trauma or stress occurs to the point of the person's mind not being able to handle the stress. The involuntary nature of it is why I say God gives us those mental escape routes; we don't create them. Dissociation is an auto-response of the brain, not a chosen one. At the point of extreme trauma, the mind splits off and literally creates another personality to handle the traumatic events while keeping the conscious brain protected from what it can't handle. Dissociation is sometimes called an "out-of-body experience." There are things that can trigger dissociation and then things that cause you to switch back to your "real mind." Switching back and forth between your conscious mind and splintered parts of your mind will automatically happen as needed (as there is trauma), and the person it is happening to is *completely unaware of the switch*. It's a God-given survival skill. He created our minds to be incomprehensibly powerful!

Dissociation is a gift that helps a person not have to *feel* the full impact of the pain and trauma she went through. So, I'm thankful I dissociated from some of the dark things that happened to me, but there is a downside. Dissociation causes you to have emotions that don't match the current circumstances. For example, when my family would drive by certain places the pastor had taken me, I'd break out in a cold sweat and start trembling, but didn't have a conscious understanding why. I would just assume that I was weird and weak, so I would do my best to hide my fearful responses.

When your mind creates different parts of itself to deal with the trauma, that trauma is then blocked from your conscious mind. It was blocked from my conscious mind; however, I did always have an underlying subconscious awareness of it. I don't know how to explain it adequately because it's complex.

For decades I had gone through things my conscious mind was somewhat but not *completely* aware of. What I *was* consciously aware of was a gnawing feeling there were dark secrets lurking inside me. I was also aware I had a major memory problem. I had many memories I could only remember in part. For instance, I'd remember all of Friday, the beginning of Saturday, but then I'd have a 10-hour block with no memories. Or, I'd remember going over to our neighbor's house and I'd remember leaving, but I couldn't remember being there. I also had a lot of emotional turmoil that didn't match the reality I was conscious of. I felt and acted like someone who had been traumatized, even though I was not consciously aware of how much I had been.

My counselor told me people who have dissociation tend to start remembering their locked away memories once they perceive they have stability and safety in many different areas of life (emotionally, physically, relationally, financially, spiritually).

Once there's perceived safety, the created compartments of your brain think maybe now they can *finally* ask for help.

For most people it happens around age 40. I was 37 when I started having clearer memories of the trauma. Flashbacks led to clearer pictures. Ultimately, I felt like I could remember a good portion of what I had blocked out for so many years. I think you only remember what you *need* to remember in order to be healed from the trauma. I didn't have to drudge up every single horror. And again, there was plenty that I'd *always* remembered. I'd only blocked out the worst of it.

Do You Have Trauma You're Unaware Of?

You might be wondering if *you* have locked away memories you're not conscious of. My response would be: you *might*. *However,* you probably have clues that let you know whether or not you do. The fruit of trauma showed up in my life even though I was not consciously aware of the source. My clues were: depression, anxiety, illogical shame, phobias, nightmares, and irrational anger about certain subjects, such as anything sexual.

Although the signs of trauma were present in me, I think my parents chalked it up to my just being high maintenance, difficult, or weak. I don't know, but they certainly weren't clued into the fact that anything of this nature was wrong. I think their own issues blinded them to mine. I'm so sad they weren't in touch with what I was going through, but forgiving them for their parental shortcomings has been a part of my process. I hope when my kids look at my parenting failures, they'll choose forgiveness, too.

Even though I wasn't conscious of a lot of the trauma I'd experienced, I always sensed it in my gut. I had many nightmares that pointed towards trauma. I had odd reactions to things. I would overreact to situations that didn't seem so bad to others, but to me felt horrible because it was linked to a traumatic memory. I battled fear all the time.

As a teenager, I remember watching an episode of Oprah Winfrey's talk show where she was interviewing people who had been abused. I thought it was odd I completely understood and related to the abuse victims. Some of them hadn't remembered it until years after they'd been through it. Apparently, a lot of abuse survivors dissociate. As I watched Oprah's show that day, I panicked because I knew that was my truth, too. I could sense there was more darkness sliding around below the surface than what I was aware of, and that it was just a matter of time before it would make its way up.

At one point, I talked to God and asked Him why I felt there was something scary and dark about myself I wasn't remembering. His response was clear and I accepted it: "You will know *what* you need to know *when* you need to know it." I trusted that God's timing was perfect and *if* and *when* I had something from my past I *needed* to deal with, He would lead me in that. So, don't jump to the conclusion that you have traumatic memories you're unaware of. However, if there are many clues and signs that you might, pray about it. Ask God to show you what you need to know. At the right time, He will.

The Process of Healing When You've Dissociated

As flashbacks began, I went to counseling. Once I went to counseling, I began unlocking emotional "cages" internally that had all sorts of locked up memories in them. In my mind's eye I could see a picture of what my mind looked like, and it resembled the over-head compartments on airplanes. I could see each overhead cab-inet door was hiding a different traumatized part of me. Some of those overhead compartments had numbers on them, represent-ing my age when they were created. Some of those compartments had names on them. I know, it's a mind-bend.

As God (through my counselor) started setting each of those captives free, one by one, I felt freer, lighter, and happier. A friend of mine who has been through something very similar says it this way: "Lies or denial feel like shackles on. Even when the truth is hard and ugly, it feels like shackles falling off." I think that most of us have a longing to be free, *truly free,* with no shackles. *We will never be truly free if we don't deal with our hurts from the past.* Please don't buy in to the whole "time heals" bit. Time doesn't *heal* anything. The Holy Spirit working through a good counselor brings healing.

My mind would feel so weird as we went through this pro-cess. I'd feel foggy, tired, and heavy. The process was pretty ex-hausting. Most of my counseling sessions were upwards of two to three hours long! It was grueling, but highly rewarding work. I left each session feeling lighter and freer than when I walked in, and after some time the payoff began to be worth the cost. (Unless you've had extreme trauma, your healing process could be much less laborious than mine.)

One of the first things God led me to deal with in counseling was the pastor friend who'd had an inappropriate relationship with me. Perhaps that's because he was still a children's pastor at our church and needed to be reported immediately. I would keep the young girls' faces he was currently working with in the front of my mind to give me courage to tell on him. Many of them were the age I was when his perverse activity began with me.

Bad Guys

This is the problem with "bad guys"; they know what "good" they have to do and be and give in order to gain the access they need to do the bad. This is only logical. Most parents aren't going to let their young daughter spend time with some older creep wearing a black trench coat hanging around in alleys. They have to *appear* to be good in order to gain the kind of trust that leads to access. I wonder if this man became a minister because of the access that title would give him to girl after girl after girl. I think it's possible, maybe even likely.

Abusive relationships are so convoluted. If you've been abused and been through healing, then you know what I mean. The knowledge of all this pastor had given me and done for me weighed on my conscious. I felt indebted. The good mixed with the bad caused so much confusion in me. I've heard the definition of wicked is good mixed in with bad to the point you can't tell the difference. That definition feels appropriate here. This man's actions, good and bad, were tangled together like a strand of last year's Christmas lights, the kind that are so tangled you should just throw the whole thing away. So I did.

Trauma followed me through life; you could say it stalked me. Because the proper boundaries and protective measures were not in place, evil found me to be an easy target. Also, once we've been traumatized, darkness sets out to wound us as many times as possible to ensure it derails our calling and destiny completely. Remember, darkness hates to see people become who God created them to be. Dark ones don't wound just for the sake of wounding; they wound to ruin, to sabotage, to thwart God's plans. You could say darkness comes to steal, kill, and destroy our callings.

So, session by session we opened the prison cells that held captive these shocked, distressed parts of me so they would come out and share what had happened to them, to me. Once I faced each little lacerated part of me, I could become one, complete, healed person (well, as much as anyone ever really can while still on earth).

God is so amazing, so genius! Think about it: He gives us free-will, which means some people are going to choose badly. The pastor *chose* to have an extremely inappropriate relationship with me. God did NOT do that to me; the pastor did. Because of free-will, it happened. However, what God DID do was block my awareness while the worst of it happened and then kept it from my awareness until just the right and perfect time when my maturity level had reached a certain point, my life circumstances were serene and safe, and I could handle it. THEN, He allowed it to come back into my consciousness and gently guided me through the process of facing it and healing from it. *THAT'S* God!! Man wounds. God heals. As long as we live in this system of free-will, this will be His way.

> *He Heals the Brokenhearted*
> *Praise the Lord! For it is good to sing praises to our God;*
> *for it is pleasant, and a song of praise is fitting.*
> *The Lord builds up Jerusalem;*
> *he gathers the outcasts of Israel.*
> *He heals the brokenhearted*
> *and binds up their wounds.*
> *(Psalm 147, ESV)*

That's God!

Questions for you to ask yourself today: Have I blamed God for any of the wounds that I've endured in my life? Might I have misplaced blame that belongs to people or Satan, but is currently being assigned to the Creator of my soul? Be careful to examine what you're believing on a subconscious level, too. Sometimes we believe things subconsciously, and we don't even realize it. You might need the help of a counselor to get down to those "underground" beliefs.

Endnotes:

1 Urban, Keith, Sarah Buxton, Deanna Bryant, and Dave Berg

. "Stupid Boy." Recorded 2006. Capitol Records Nashville.

2 McCarthy, Tom, dir. 2015. *Spotlight. O*pen Road Films.

3 Edmund Burke. Accessed March 28, 2017.

https://www.brainyquote.com/quotes/quotes/e/edmundburk377528.html

CHAPTER 7

Cloudy With A Chance Of Reign

"When you possess great treasures within you and try to tell others of them, seldom are you believed." [1]

Quirky Kid

I was a quirky kid. Quirky sounds so much nicer than weird, doesn't it? I never quite felt like I fit...*anywhere*. Even when I pretended to be a black belt in karate or when I wore my Michael Jackson pin, I just never could fully feel at home among humans. I felt most comfortable around my church friends, but even there I knew the sound of my drum was different.

One day at school when I was in sixth grade, I observed my teacher had some wall space about the width of my desk that was unused. This blank wall space was nestled between two filing cabinets, and it had my name written all over it.

I was always getting in trouble for talking in class. Like so many kids, I hated school! The only redemptive quality it had was being able to talk to other kids. I didn't discriminate either. I enjoyed talking to anyone and everyone from all walks of life... still do. God bless my teachers. They were always trying to seat me next to someone I wouldn't be likely to talk to, but I liked talking to *everyone*. Bless their hearts.

I'm sure that's why my teacher immediately said, "YES!" when I asked if I could move my desk into that spot against the wall between the filing cabinets...away from all the other kids. I don't think she stopped to wonder why in the world I would want to do that. She was just glad I wouldn't have anyone to talk to!

I wanted to do that because I was bored out of my mind, and that space called to the creative entrepreneur in me. When I saw that space, I saw a place where I could be hidden enough to be creative with my time. A space that would allow me mentally to escape the prison of school. Specifically, I saw a place where I could run my make-believe businesses without anyone being able to see. So. Quirky.

So, I moved my desk into the space and set up shop. I brought office supplies from home and arranged them on my desk so I could look like a real boss. I put things up on the wall and the filing cabinets to make it feel more like a real office (things like inspirational quotes from Zig Ziglar and pictures of Jonathon Livingston Seagull). Then, when everyone was doing school work and not paying attention to me, I would make pretend phone calls and type on my pretend typewriter. I was running an imaginary handbag business right there from the sixth-grade classroom. I created purses and sold them all over the world. I was also a motivational speaker, and I would correspond with my make-believe clients about coming to speak for them.

Growing up my dad made me listen to a lot of Zig Ziglar, Brian Tracy, Charles Stanley, Tony Robbins, Chuck Swindoll, and James Dobson, among many others. I acted like I hated listening, but I always learned something and secretly enjoyed it. While most kids were playing games and riding their bikes, I was listening to motivational speakers and preachers. Not normal.

Because of all that teaching, I developed a desire to inspire others through speaking. Actually, I think I had that desire in me from my creation, and my dad was just nurturing a gift that was already in me. I loved the thought of inspiring others to be the best version of themselves. I loved listening to speakers who did that for me and relished the thought of encouraging people and giving them hope for the future, inspiring them to be their best. I still do.

So, at school I was running a pretend business and corresponding with fake clients, while at home I was speaking to pretend audiences. I would force my sweet little brother to film me with our huge JVC VHS camera while I spoke to pretend groups. That way I could watch the films afterward to see how I could improve. Kind of like football teams who get together to watch films of themselves playing so they can see how to improve their games. Only there was no audience, and my third-grade brother was the videographer. *Quirky.*

Cast as the Leading Lady

While in elementary school I also decided that I really wanted to have a cast. You know the kind you get when you break a limb? I'd seen people come to school with them, and I was intrigued. I knew that this would require me to break a limb, and

I was fine with that...as long as I got a cast. So, my brother and some of our friends set out to break my leg.

I was good with breaking my leg, but I didn't want it to hurt, *obviously*! We put the cushions from our couch on the ground under our tallest tree. I climbed to the highest point I could and jumped, aiming for the cushions so I wouldn't hurt myself, of course. Sadly, I was unable to break my leg no matter how much I jumped. To this day, I've never been fortunate enough to have a cast.

Besides wanting a cast, I also desperately wanted to fly. I loved the feeling of wind in my face, flying like a bird, not in an airplane. I'd learned about birds and how their wings worked for keeping them in flight. I concluded all I needed were some wings, and I'd be set. The garbage can lids looked a lot like wings to me. So, I took two lids and climbed up onto the roof of our house. I looked at the view from our roof, and thought, "Gosh, what a beautiful day for my first flight!" I put my arms out to my sides, holding a lid in each hand. I jumped and began flapping as hard as I could. Sadly, that didn't work either. I've never made the claim I was the brightest bear in the forest, but I did have guts and determination!

I currently have this quote hanging in my living room:

"I do not intend to tiptoe through life only to arrive safely at death." [2]

I love that. I live that. Always have.

Big Vic

I've also gone after injustice with a lot of chutzpah, especially when I was a kid. I hated injustice, passionately. When I was a kid and I saw something unjust, I would often act or speak before I thought. While I was in my healing process, I began thinking a lot about that gutsy little girl. Throughout adulthood I'd seen glimpses of her occasionally, but it seemed that her fire had dimmed quite a bit.

One hot afternoon I was in my counselor's warm, pretty office with hues of plum and gold around the room. I looked around and saw flowers, angel figurines, a clock so small I could barely read the time on it, a box of Kleenex, and a plant.

I sat down on the flaxen love seat and begin to stare out the quaint double French doors into the yard. My gaze became fixed on a large Juniper bush that reminded me of my childhood home. (Well, one of them; there were many. This was the house where I'd lived when I jumped out of the tree and off the roof.) I thought of the house I lived in from third grade to eighth grade before my grandmother evicted us. Anyway, the house had these ugly Juniper bushes that ran straight through the middle of the front yard. The oddly-placed bushes ended at a large towering pine tree of some variety. My mom, who isn't passionate about anything, passionately hated those Juniper bushes. I'm not sure why.

As I stared at these Juniper bushes waiting for my counselor to get the fan for me (I'm always hot) and get settled in, my mind drifted away from the uncomfortable subjects that would be broached that day. My subconscious medicates me byway of daydreams. I thought about that house with the Juniper bushes and the pine tree, and how my friend Stacey, my brother, and I created a fort under that pine. The Junipers acted as the fort's walls and the Pine's branches, being just the right height for our child-sized frames, doubled as our ceiling.

It was in that fort one hot, California, afternoon that Stacey told me her dad was a "son of a (expletive)." That language made me extremely uncomfortable, as we didn't cuss in my house growing up. It also made me uncomfortable because I *adored* her dad! Aside from my own dad, he was my favorite. He had a super cool, red Jeep that he'd take us out in. The top off, wind in my hair, he drove faster than he ought….it was the best! I thought *he* was the best. He even picked us up early from school one day to take us to lunch in his cool Jeep. Then, he took us home for an official ditch day. *So cool.*

Because my opinion of Stacey's dad was so high, her calling him such a derogatory name, hurt my heart. "Why are you saying that, Stacey?" I asked. After all, she'd always adored her dad, too.

"My dad has been having an affair!" She blurted out. "He's been cheating on my mom with one of her best friends. I hate him! He's a son of a (expletive)!" She said with fiery pain.

I was stunned. Big Vic, as he was called (perhaps because of his five-foot, three-inch height), was having an affair? I felt betrayed, too. I loved him. I loved his Jeep. This was terrible news. We sat in silence for a minute. Stacey said, "My mom told us what was going on, and then my dad got home. So, I ran down to our fort to get away from him. I never want to see him again!"

"Well, you can stay here as long as you want!" I declared with adult-like authority. "How can we make him pay?" I asked her. "I'll help you hurt him if you want. I will, I mean it." And I *did*, mean it. I was a very loyal friend. I could see the heartache she felt. My heart ached right along with hers. We sat stewing and contemplating a few different options of how to make Big Vic suffer for what he'd done. The details were hard to map out for our 12-year-old brains, but it was comforting to consider revenge. My ideas made Stacey laugh, and that made me feel good.

All of a sudden, "Stacey?"

We froze as we heard Big Vic's voice calling in the fairly close distance.

"Stacey, come back. We need to talk."

Stacey stood up nervously and looked for a place to hide. The tears that had dried were now re-forming in her eyes. Seeing her distress enraged me.

"Go away, loser. She doesn't want to talk to you!" I bravely yelled from behind the Juniper bushes that were as tall as I was, so he couldn't see me *at all*.

"Rachel? Is Stacey with you?" Big Vic asked, as he was now just about 15 feet away on the sidewalk. I was peering straight at his promiscuous face through the branches. Big Vic stood facing the fort with his eyes darting around, looking for us. How did he know it was *me* who yelled? I'd hoped to remain anonymous while I let into him.

Determining he couldn't place my voice *conclusively,* I continued. The fact that he was standing in front of *my* house and *my* fort and knew *my* voice never crossed my mind. Remember, I said I had chutzpah, not brilliance.

"You're a cheater! You're an idiot, and we hate you, Vic! If you were my dad, I would never talk to you again for my whole life! Do you know how horrible you are? We really, really hate you. God is going to punish you. I hope you know that! And we *don't* forgive you. We never will." I yelled with disdain and pre-teen, loyal hormones pumping. Stacey was nodding along affirmatively as I yelled, which made me feel I'd done well.

Then big Vic's voice came back, "Rachel, I know that you're

mad and hurt, but you don't know the whole story."

Don't know the whole story? What is there to know? You cheated, my best friend is hurt, I'm hurt, and that's all I need to know! Now I was really angry! That was his way of saying if I knew some other piece of information, I wouldn't be so mad that he'd cheated. Nothing could have been further from the truth.

"No, Vic, I don't need to know anything else other than you betrayed your family and now I hate you for it. By the way, you don't even know who this is. It may not be Rachel. Anyway, Stacey doesn't want to see you ever again!" I said as I looked at Stacey's disturbed face that was still nodding "yes" to me.

Big Vic spoke again. "Rachel, tell Stacey that she needs to come home. I need to talk to her. I'm sorry that you girls are hurt. Some day you'll understand. Tell Stacey, okay?" I looked down at Stacey who now had tears streaming down her face as she collapsed from her squatting position onto her bottom, into the Juniper. Snap went a branch. Snap went our pre-teen hearts.

It was such a sad and horrible moment. I remember the smell of the Juniper oil and Pine, and the way the sweat was pouring off my body as the dust beneath our feet rose through the air like smoke from a fire. I remember the unbearable dejection on my friend's face and in my heart. Her pain felt like injustice to me. She was a victim to her dad's choice to cheat. I hated that. That day in my counselor's office I thought about Stacey's pain, and it somehow helped me to feel less alone in mine.

I Asked, That's How

There's a fine line between stupidity and chutzpah. I walked that line. When I wanted something, I went for it. When I saw injustice, I tried to nail it to the wall. I've always had this driving desire for things to be the way God intended for them to be. When I saw an opportunity to improve my life or the lives of those I've loved, I jumped at it, sometimes literally. I've failed a lot. I've flapped my garbage can wings with all my might, but still fallen to the ground. However, I've also received a lot of justice simply because I had the guts to go for it.

One time there was a concert I wanted to attend, but I thought it'd be more fun with a bunch of people. So, I asked around and got about 30 people to go to the concert with my husband and me.

I purchased the tickets for everyone so we could all sit together in one big group. When we arrived at the arena and got to our seats, there was a huge, permanent Budweiser sign blocking our view. The artists came on stage, and we could only see them from the waist down.

Since I'd coordinated this outing and purchased the tickets, I felt terrible! I had no way of knowing that sign was going to be there, obviously, but I felt responsible. So, I got up during the first act and went to find an arena employee. I told them the situation and asked if they could possibly move our group of 30 people to better seats where we could actually see.

They said, "Yes." I went back and motioned to everyone to get up and follow me. Some of them seemed a little annoyed about getting up in the middle of a performance. Thirty people moving at the same time was quite disruptive to everyone around us, too. Nonetheless, they led us back into the arena, all the way up to the front, pointing to a section that was roped off right by the stage and the stairs the artists used to go on and off the stage.

"You and your people may occupy this whole section."

So we went from terrible seats to some of the best seats in the house. Now suddenly everyone was patting me on the back and happy that I'd disrupted their show.

"How did you get these seats for us?" they asked in amazement.

My response, "I asked."

Sometimes it's as simple as asking for something. Sometimes you just have to try, to go for it. You have to get those garbage can lids and head on up to the roof because you *might* be able to fly. You might not be able to, but you won't know unless you try.

I think our callings will require us to have a lot of faith along with some chutzpah, some guts. If we're not willing to risk... if we're not willing to fail...if we're not willing to ask...if we're not willing to look stupid... I don't think we'll become the fullest, best versions of ourselves, and I definitely don't think we'll live in our promised lands.

Thankfully, as I've gotten healthier, I've found I can be led by God and walk more on the wise side of chutzpah. I've also realized a lot of the dreams in the heart of that young, quirky girl were actually from God. Those dreams were indicators about who He'd created me to be. I was compelled to yell at Big Vic because I was created to be a voice that spoke out for injustice. I wanted to put my desk over between those filing cabinets because my calling was going to be very unique and because I was going to run my own business. I wasn't created to "fit in."

As I continued in counseling and got healthier, I felt like I regained the fire that had made me attempt flying, yell at an adulterous man, and get a concert coordinator to move me and my 30 friends to more desirable seats. The return of fearless, audacious, idiosyncratic Rachel is one of my favorite things about counseling. I returned to myself.

Cloudy with a Chance Of Reign

As a kid, I liked re-arranging my bedroom furniture. It was something I could control. Junior high embodied gross, deplorable events for me, as it might have for you, too. I've yet to meet the person who says, "Seventh grade, boy those were the days!" You probably wouldn't label junior high as the peak of your life. Moving my furniture around was like pushing pause on torment that a seventh-grade girl experiences. The newly arranged furniture felt like a fresh start...in life.

This one night I couldn't shake the melancholy like I normally could. As I pushed my dresser inch by strenuous inch, I breezed through my laundry list of dramas in prayer, although I wasn't completely convinced God would help me feel better. I had no other potential solution, so I gave it a shot.

"God, things are horrible for me! My family has *no* money, and at school I'm surrounded by rich kids. Our electricity was turned off, and then magically was turned on again. I think my dad borrowed money from someone again. The phone has been cut off, and on a day I was expecting a call from a boy! Please, God, help me to think of a lie to tell him about why it was turned off! My brother read my diary to this same boy, so I'm already embarrassed! My parents are so tense because of money problems. We eat a lot of beans and cornbread, and I'm so tired of that. My mom's entire family has cut off their relationship with us because of a financial transaction that has gone bad, *I think*. No one will tell me what really happened. I miss my cousins! I don't understand why our own family would ever turn their backs on us. At school, I can't pay attention in class. I'm worried about my parents, and I'm always trying to think of ways to help them.

My grades aren't very good. The Mexican girls with the big hair keep pushing me around and threatening me in PE. I'm scared every day. Then, worst of all, my best friend has completely abandoned me at school. I hate going not knowing who I can eat lunch with from day to day. I feel so lonely. I feel like everyone is walking away from me. What's wrong with me? Why don't these people want to be in my life? Help me to feel better, be smarter, and more fun to be with! PLEASE! I feel so embarrassed all time. I'm scared. I can't stop thinking about scary things that could happen to me. I have nightmares almost every night about things I can't tell anyone about. I don't even know if You care or are listening to me, but if You are, I need You to help my family and me. In Jesus' Name, Amen."

Needing a break from re-arranging, I slid my back down my closet wall and plopped onto its floor. Then, under a closet shelf I spotted something my step-grandma gave me four or so Christmases ago. She'd given all her "real" grandkids things like toys and clothes and pretty tea sets. I remember them opening box after box. Then, *finally*, there was *one* with my name on it! I was hoping for Tropical Barbie or a sapphire ring. By the size of the box, it looked like it might be both! I tore into the Christmas wrapping paper excitedly and found a green, paperback Bible with a picture of a candle on the front and a big, round, yellow sale price tag still on it: $1.99. I faked a sneeze to hide my tears.

"Thanks, a Bible, wow, that's great. I'll add it to the stack of six Bibles already in my bedroom." I thought. But then I felt guilty for feeling that way. I've always been one that has a heavy conscience when I do the slightest thing wrong. Not because I don't think I'm forgiven, but because I so wanted to please and honor God. If I were honest though, I hated that gift, and resented my step-grandma for treating my brother and me like second class citizens. She did nothing to hide her partiality, and it was hurtful.

Fast forward a few years and I'm in my closet picking up the Bible *I never wanted*. I felt the sting of rejection again as I looked at its cover. It was a terrible gift for a kid. It wasn't even a hard cover, and she'd left the $1.99 sticker on it! It's like she *wanted* us to know we weren't valuable to her. Message received!

I remember getting into the car that Christmas Eve night and my dad saying, "You got the best gift there tonight! What an honor that grandma Norma thought you would like a Bible for Christmas!" That was bologna, and he knew it. She wasn't trying to honor me. He was always trying to put a positive spin on the terrible situations we found ourselves in, and I loved him for it. He tried. But then, my mom acknowledged we must be disappointed with our gifts, and she was sorry. I loved *her* for *that*.

I must have been around third grade the year she gave us those cheap, green paperbacks. Now, in seventh grade I began flipping through its pages for the first time. I opened to Psalms and started to read. I don't remember which Psalm. I only remember what happened when I started reading. I remember the words leaping off the page and penetrating my soul in some sort of supernatural, captivating, life-giving way. I began to cry as God made Himself known to me through King David's words. It was as if they were my own words, expressing the ache in my own soul. I felt like God was saying, "I see. I know. I'm here."

But THEN, a *literal* cloud filled my closet and bedroom and God Himself settled in that closet floor with me. Joy... no, euphoria...shot from my feet to my scalp and it swirled around like a surge of sugar into my bloodstream. My mouth was gaping open as I experienced God's presence with utter awe. It was a tangible experience, a cloud I could see and touch, *literally*. At that time of my life, I had no idea that God had revealed Himself this way in the Bible as well.

To my sheer delight, I once heard singer/songwriter Lenny Kravitz on "Oprah's Master's Class" describe an encounter He had with God that was almost identical to mine. He recounted a cloud settling in a room where he and another child were as they read Scripture together. He talked about how he knew that was God's presence, even though he'd not known anything about God before that. He and his friend had cried, too. It's cool to hear of someone else having a similar, miraculous encounter like that, and as kid, no less. God's comforting presence enveloped me in that cloud, and I knew He'd heard every word I'd just spoken to Him. But somehow, I also knew He'd heard every word I'd *never* spoken.

As I sat in "The Cloud," I felt the romanticism of being fully known and accepted. God does not compartmentalize like I do. When He sees me, He sees every part of me. From that experience, I gained more than I can articulate. I believe we each have an aching, cavernous desire to be fully known yet still accepted. In Him alone will we have this desire met. No human being will ever truly know all of us. Sometimes we don't even fully know ourselves. That privilege is reserved for God alone. His presence lured healing sobs out of me. I kept crying out, "You're real! You're real! You're real! Thank You! Thank You! Thank You! You're real! Thank You!"

I took a deep breath in and sure enough, the scent of wild honey was in the cloud. I jarred up some of that wild honey in hopes of giving some of it to people that I loved. I so badly wanted them to taste this supernatural substance. I wanted others to share in the joy I was experiencing. I wanted them to get to feel His cloudy presence on their skin, the way that I was. "If they get to feel His presence like this, they'll love Him like I do," I thought.

Blessed are the pure in heart for they shall *see* God.

Encountering God changed me to the core of my soul that night. No matter what I did or where I went, I felt the coolness of His cloudy presence on my skin. Deep inside my gut I knew this: God is with me. When Scripture tells us God is near to the brokenhearted, it means He's literally, *near* to the brokenhearted. After this cloudy night I knew that on whole new level.

Normals Don't Get It

This is what I longed for you to know: He was with you too. Have you ever been hurt, felt broken, cast down, rejected, or victimized? If so, God was near to you in that pain. Even if you've not always realized He was near, He was. God's nearness is such a blessing to us wounded warriors. We, who have been hurt, have had a chance to see and experience God in a way others haven't, in a way they're not even welcomed to. There's a kind of encounter that's reserved only for the brokenhearted. We may wish our lives could be without pain; but if they were, we'd have to forfeit some of our proximity to God. It's a trade-off.

That night I experienced God's promise of being near to the brokenhearted in a literal, tangible way. And, may I just say He had me at "hello." I was so smitten with God after this encounter. He was sweeter and more real to me than I could have imagined was possible. I so want you to know that about God. *God* wants you to know that. He's real. He's kind and gentle and at the same time perfectly strong. He loves you and cares about every detail of your life. He's always been with you, even when you were in that dark place you don't like to talk about. You know that heinous place you've not told a soul about? He was with you and loved you in the middle of *that* place.

I tried to tell a few people about my experience with "The Cloud," and they were completely unimpressed, or maybe just flat out didn't believe me. It was disheartening. They gave me fake, pacifying responses as if to say, "Oh, you have such a good imagination" or, "That's really nice, sweetie." Or the worst response was, "You're so cute!" which is code for, "You're being creative, but not honest."

I guess some things God gives us are *just for us*. No one else will be able to fully grasp the significance or power of God's activity in our lives. Others won't even believe it. That used to frustrate me because I so badly wanted others to understand His love, His presence, His power and how it all had affected me... how it could affect *them*. Learning that truth the hard way is why I appreciate this quote:

> *"When you possess great treasures within you and try to tell others of them, seldom are you believed."* [3]

I believe God desires to reveal Himself to each of us individually. He doesn't just want us to see Him as someone else conveys Him to us. I also believe some people who call themselves Christians have very little faith about what they believe God can or will do. How sad for them. I hope you have a view of God that is without limits. Be assured of the fact He can do whatever He wants, whenever He wants!

I love that God did not hold back from doing something supernatural in my life just because I was unaware this sort of thing could happen. My ignorance or lack of instruction on the supernatural did not hinder His supernatural activity in my life. I was raised in churches that never talked about supernatural occurrences. They believed they had ceased along with the death of the first century church. However, our opinions do not change His reality. He is who He is, regardless of what we think. No person's or denomination's lack of belief would in any way change the truth of the what happened to me that night.

The pure in heart have seen God, or at least *have had the chance to.* Wounded ones have pain that caused God to draw near to us. He has revealed Himself to us in a special, tender way that those who don't have a heart for Him and who have not been devastated know nothing of. Perhaps that's why when I would try to explain my encounters with God to a painless, average person, they could not really appreciate it. "Normal" people have never experienced the lows I have. However, they've also never experienced the highs, the "God is near" moments. That fact causes me to feel so sorry for the "Normals."

How unfortunate it must be never to have been wounded to the point of seeing God draw near in a unique way! I can only imagine how dreadful their lives are. I pity them. The only thing that seems worse than being a "Normal" is being a wounded one, but *not* seeing God when He drew near. Being brokenhearted, but missing God's presence, not accepting His gifts, blaming Him for what Satan did...*that* would be even worse than being "Normal."

Rotten Fruit

As blessed as I was by these special moments with God, there was still a lot of rotten fruit in my life. Even though I'd experienced God's presence in such a sweet way, I was depressed. In fact, seeing God made me want to go be with Him *permanently*. Depression was only an underlying issue for my early teen years. But by the time that I was 17, I was fully depressed.

I'd gone to a counselor, but it wasn't helpful at all. Later I would find out the counselor had an on-again, off-again sexual relationship with the pastor who'd abused me! Yep, you read that right. The counselor that counseled me had a romantic relationship with my abuser. Good grief! *No wonder* she wasn't helpful to me! That fact still blows my mind!

You know what's so cool though? Even at that young age, when I was still so young and immature, God showed me during a counseling session that I needed NOT to share anything else with that counselor. I remember her asking me a question about that pastor, then hearing God speak into my spirit, "She's asking you that question because of her own personal curiosity. Don't answer her. Don't give her any more information." So I didn't.

I ended up switching counselors. Still counseling wasn't too helpful then because I was trying to deal with depression while not revealing any of the abuse I'd endured, at least the part I was aware of at that point. That's not very effective. I used to avoid telling my counselor about the abuse I'd been through because I didn't want to depress her. I think that brings a whole new meaning to the word co-dependent! Even without telling my counselor everything, counseling was moderately helpful the second time around. At least counselor number two wasn't sleeping with my perpetrator! It could have been so much more helpful had I told the whole truth to counselor number two. But it would be 20 more years before I would.

We're All Happy, Act Accordingly

I tried to hide my depression, as I believed "good Christians" shouldn't be depressed, and I really wanted to be a good Christian! I borrowed that belief about depression from my local church. Perhaps you are blessed to go to a church where people are real about their emotional struggles. I'm sure there's a church out there that is real, *somewhere*. No one, not one person, as I was growing up at church had *ever* acknowledged being depressed, and that only exaggerated my sense of shame. So, I'd put on a myriad of masks and played parts as needed. Happy girl, friendly girl, confident girl - whatever the situation called for.

Do you remember Phoebe Snow's song "No Show Tonight"?

> *There'll be no show tonight and no, no*
> *The music won't sound right*
> *The audience is being impolite*
> *And I can't act tonight, don't make me*
> *I can't act tonight.* [4]

I remember that song ringing so true as there were many days when I just couldn't act like a good, happy Christian. I couldn't put on the show. The audience was being impolite.

In John Mayer's song "Born and Raised" he says,

> *Then all at once it gets hard to take.*
> *It gets hard to fake what I won't be.*
> *'Cause one of these days I'll be born and raised,*
> *and it's such a waste to grow up lonely.* [5]

Pretending to be something you're not is very lonely, and some days I just couldn't play the part!

On the days I couldn't *act*, I'd hide away so I could maintain my secrets. I was a good actress most days. I had to become a good actress in order to keep putting one foot in front of the other and just keep doing life. I have a theory that most professional actors/actresses have been traumatized and have dissociated. That's how they so naturally can play many different parts. They've done it all their lives. I'd certainly done it all of mine. Shouldn't I get some sort of award for that, perhaps a trophy or a sash or *something*? I'd played my roles so effectively that no one around me ever asked, "Are you okay?" or "Are you depressed?" "Everything okay in there?" My youth was one big game and because I'd fooled everyone into thinking that I was happy, I'd won. Or so I thought - until January 1997.

Question 1: Have you "played a part" at any time in your life? Are you still playing a part and not being sincere and authentic? Ask God to show you if you need to be more authentic in any area of your life.

Question 2: Have you ever experienced God's presence in a unique way? If you have, take a minute to consciously remember just how amazing that was. It's possible that you have been in His presence, but you didn't recognize the presence as being God.

Question 3: What were some of your childhood dreams and aspirations? Who did you dream of becoming? It's possible you should revisit your childhood desires for clues to who God has created you to be.

Endnotes:

1 Coelho, Paulo. *The Alchemist.* New York: HarperCollins, 1998.

2 Author unknown.

3 Coelho, Paulo. *The Alchemist.* New York: HarperCollins, 1998.

4 Snow, Phoebe. "No Show Tonight." Recorded 1974. Shelter Records.

5 Mayer, John. "Born & Raised." Recorded 2012. Columbia Records.

CHAPTER 8

Meeting Father John

Darkness has a hunger that's insatiable
And lightness has a call that's hard to hear
I wrapped my fear around me like a blanket
I sailed my ship of safety till I sank it
I'm crawling on your shores [1]

"Are you depressed?" Father John asked.

"Me?" I asked with genuine shock.

"Yes."

"Well, I mean my grandmother's dying. I think anyone would feel sad right now."

"Yes, agreed. But that's not what I'm talking about. Are you *depressed*?"

Silence. I'm stunned. I just met this man a couple days ago. He was my grandma's Episcopalian Priest. He came to visit her in the hospital and ended up spending quite a bit of time talking with our family in the days leading up to her death. I'd spent my whole life attempting to come across as someone different than I was, and it had always worked. I thought I had perfected the craft of looking "okay" and cheerful even when I wasn't. So why was he asking me this? How could he possibly know? What had I done wrong?

"Um." I said with *total class.*

As we stood on opposite sides of my dying grandmother's bed, I avoided making eye contact. I thought I'd been acting "fine"; therefore, Father John shouldn't know I'm depressed! I've been acting on cue, not missing any lines, saying all the right, appropriate normal things. Why is he asking me if I'm depressed?! I'm annoyed. I don't want to answer, but I must make him happy, as is my co-dependent way.

"Um." I said again because the first "um" wasn't enough.

I'm all of 20 years old and have already been married for two months. My 20-year old, handsome, husband is staring at me, no doubt wondering what I'm going to say and maybe wondering why he's asking the question to begin with. I look at my husband, hoping he'll read my mind and answer for me, but he'd yet to perfect that skill. I look down at dying, intubated grandma, and then up at Father John.

Finally, "Yes, I am depressed." I said. "I'm trying not to be though!" I began with a speech I'd internally memorized and repeated to myself. "I know I have a lot to be thankful for, and I'm trying to focus on that. Life's not always easy, but it's always good. God is good. I know I'm a lot better off than some people, that's for sure." I successfully regurgitated some sort of flowery imagery I'd heard somewhere, made note of, and gone on to memorize. I tried to believe it, too.

Father John just stared at me, listening as if he knew the truth of the matter regardless of what I said. I felt like he could see past my "presentation" straight into my soul. This both horrified and delighted me. That's the first time I'd had this experience, where I'm talking to someone and it felt as though he was peering straight through me. It was like my soul was naked when this person was around. I'd later learn it's part of a discernment gift mix - the ability to see what's not obvious. I'd also discover I too had that gift; but because so much of my reality did not line up with what I needed it to be, I learned at a young age to silence that voice of discernment. When you discern something is really wrong, but the adults around you are saying "Shhh, everything is fine," you tell the inner voice to sit down and shut up! It must be quiet if you are to stay sane.

To be on the receiving side of one of these soul-penetrating stares is a magical, gratifying, terrifying, disturbing, and calming experience. Have you ever experienced it, when someone sees into your soul? I hope you have. I'm glad I've had that experience a few times in my life. It's such an interesting feeling. The experience of being truly seen, despite my facade, is one of the many glimpses I've had of heaven. It reveals one tiny facet of God's character. God can see straight to the truth, no matter what kind of screens we put up. That day, so could Father John.

"Uh huh." He said nodding along as I talked as if wanting to be gracious, yet not buying anything I said. "Well," he said, "sometimes coming out of depression has nothing to do with trying harder." Instantly I felt some relief from the guilt about being depressed. He continued, "Would it be okay if I prayed with you about this depression? I'd like to pray for you to be healed."

Indignation rose up in me. Pray for me to be healed?! Oh, I've prayed until I'm blue in the face! I've asked God to take away the sadness, to help me feel normal! I've prayed!! I felt agitated that he thought so little of this heavy cloak of darkness that was over me that he could just come and pray it away! My heart sank into my stomach as I longed for it to be that simple. I put up a wall to protect myself from the inevitable disappointment that his prayers would do nothing for me. Yet there was a tiny part of me that whispered, "What if it helps?" Fear of predetermined failure shushed that whisper.

I feel a little trapped by his request, like I had to say yes. My mind held up to itself flashcards of all the things I'd done to "feel better." The flashcards read:

1. Exercised

2. Eaten right

3. Gone to counseling

4. Taken antidepressants

5. Prayed, and then prayed more, and then continued praying

6. Read self-help books

7. Tried hard to think happy thoughts, blah, blah, blah.

As I thought about all I'd already done to be well, I felt annoyed by the arrogance of his suggestion that *his* prayer for me would help. However, I figured I had nothing to lose, other than some wasted time, which I was sure it would be.

"Sure, I guess you can pray for me. If YOU want to."

He didn't seem put-off by my lack of enthusiasm, and my making it clear I was doing him some sort of favor by letting him pray for me.

"Great. What's a good day and time for you? I'd like to schedule a time to come to your home when both you and your husband can be there."

Seriously? He was going to nail me down to make an actual appointment right here on the spot! This guy was rather pushy! I decided to go ahead and just set up a date and time in order to get him off my back, knowing I would cancel it later.

I pulled out my Hallmark Greeting Card miniature, paper calendar and said, "Oooookkkaaaayyyyy, how about a week from Thursday at 2:00? I get out of class at noon that day, and Marshall gets off work at 1:00."

I thought, he had better not expect me to rearrange my schedule for him! I don't even want to do this. I'm just trying to be nice. If he can't do it that day and time, I simply will not make it work any other time.

"Yes, 2 o'clock Thursday, February 10th. Yes, that works great. What's your address?"

"Well, we live about 35 minutes from here." I said, hoping to discourage him.

"No problem. Write down your address for me."

He reached over and tore out the mailing card from a nearby magazine and handed it to me along with a pen.

The horrible smell of the hospital where my grandma lay dying was making me nauseous; or maybe it was Father John. I quickly wrote down my address, handed it to him, then slipped out to get some fresh air. I was annoyed both that my husband didn't read my mind and that he stayed back to continue talking to Father John as I went outside.

I made my way down the elevator, past the old lady volunteers who sat at the entrance, and out the double doors to the cool, California air. I took a breath, but it probably looked more like a gasp to those passing by. What had I just agreed to? If I was honest with myself, *deep down inside*, I felt a tiny bit of hopeful expectation with Father John. I started to see his confidence as a sign *maybe* he knew something I didn't know, rather than seeing it as arrogance. I wrote our appointment down in my little paper calendar - February 10th at 2 o'clock - and I underlined it. I tried not to let myself feel too much hope, because I didn't want to experience the letdown of another failed attempt to be free. I pressed down fear and sadness, put on my game face, and mustered up courage (from God only knows where), pulled my sweatshirt up over my nose to block the hospital smells, and headed back inside.

Good Ol' Winnie

Grandma died the next day, and it wasn't a sad thing. She was very grouchy and pretty miserable to visit. I was glad not to have to make any more trips from Clovis to Madera just to hear her tell me how incorrect my grammar was, is-ugh I can hear her corrective voice even now. The first time she met my fiancé (who would later become my husband), she asked him, "What are you studying in school, young man?"

"I am a liberal studies major, ma'am. I am going to be a teacher." He said with a sparkle in his eye and proud grandeur in his voice. Grandma Winnie had been an educator, so he was happy to tell her of his choice to go into that field. He knew they could connect on that subject.

"'Ma'am' is slang, young man, and you're not a Liberal Studies major. You're a person. If you're going to speak with such a low level, slang vocabulary, how do you expect to educate children effectively? You may call me Mrs. Machock, not ma'am. Do you even play the piano?"

My poor fiancé looked like a deer in headlights. "Um..." he said.

"UM? Who taught you to speak? UM? Where's your confidence? The children will not respect an insecure, skittish teacher! You'll need much refining before you dare step foot into a classroom. So *do you*?"

"Do I what?"

"Do I what? *DO YOU PLAY THE PIANO?*" Grandma was doing the closest thing to yelling that she was capable of doing while wearing an oxygen mask because of years of filling her lungs with tar.

"No ma'am. I'm, I'm sorry. Mrs. Machock, no, no I don't. I don't play the piano."

I watched my fiancé as he's being eaten alive by Ol' Granny Winnie. I wanted to rescue him, but there was no rescuing that would take place. That's like saying you wanted to rescue the tsunami victims as the wave is directly above their heads. It was just not happening. I tried to warn him about her, but until you were in the presence of Winifred Machock, you were never fully prepared. She was so unique.

She wouldn't allow us to say we needed to go to the restroom. For some reason, she found that to be offensive. Even worse was saying "bathroom." She'd say, "Are you going to be taking a bath? Then why did you say you're going to the bath-room?" Instead we had to say, "Grandmother, I need to micturate."

My grandmother let out a sigh with a condescending tone as my then fiancé spoke. She was famous for it. "*You don't even play the piano and you expect to be a teacher?* You will *not* be successful as an educator until you learn how to play the piano! You've got the fingers for it, slender and long. I'm disappointed you've not had the discipline to learn. You also need to learn to speak correctly before you expect to teach children."

At this point, my sweet, young, fiancé just sat stunned, silently. He could already see that no response would be received, nor appreciated. He's very perceptive and wise and can assimilate into any environment quickly. That's part of what drew me to him. He had already learned his silence was his protection here.

Grandma then turned to me and said she had some pants and a sweater that no longer fit her and she thought they'd be perfect for me. "They're on my bed for you to try on. They'll be just darling on you! Put them on and then come let me see them on you."

"Yes, grandma," I said as I got up to show expeditious obedience. Frankly, I was scared of her, even at 19 years old. I headed into her room that reeked of cigarettes and musk. I saw a pair of white, TINY, skin-tight, size 4, faux leather "hot pants" that were probably made the year that I was born. I also saw a chocolate brown Champion sweatshirt that had been cut up the center and had lace sown along the cut. It had flowery, peach and gold colored fabric appliqué all over the front and back of the brown sweatshirt. The appliqué was outlined with gold glitter glue.

Trying on this outfit was going to create quite the show. My mother was visiting grandma with us, and I anticipated how she and my fiancé would respond to this "cute" outfit grandma thought would be "just darling on me." I SQUEEZED my 108 pound, five-foot, six-inch, stick-skinny body into the hot pants that zipped in the back and I could *barely* get the zipper up. I then slid on this hideous, majorly old-lady, cigarette smelling "sweater/sweatshirt" and looked into her mirror. I crossed my legs to keep from having an accident, covered my mouth and shook from laughing so hard. I kept trying to go out to show them, but I couldn't stop laughing long enough to go.

"Rachel? What's taking so long? Do they fit?" I heard grandma barking in an annoyed, smoker's voice from her permanent position on her flaming, fire-engine red couch. I had to stop laughing to try to answer her. With a shaky voice, I called out, "Yeah."

"What? Speak up!" she said.

"Uh huh." That was all I could get out without her knowing that I was laughing.

"Well, come show us!"

I started to walk out, *trying* to put on my serious face. Grandma would not be happy if I was laughing. I walked to the edge of the living room where my mom and fiancé could see me, but my grandma's back was to me. I saw my fiancé burst out in laughter at the sight of me, then quickly put his face into his hands and turned to the side to try to hide his response from grandma. My mom squeezed her lips together and was also trying to keep from disrespecting my grandmother by laughing at the ensemble. My grandma motioned for me to come around and stand before her. I crept up, but then had to step back because I was cracking up. Finally, I was able to get my composure enough to step into her view.

Winifred gave her opinion. *"Oh, yes! That IS adorable! Wow, you've got the body for those pants, don't you? And the sweatshirt...it's you! Brown, peach, and gold do go nicely together, don't they? Clearly, they're in your color palate! Marshall, what do you think?"*

Marshall couldn't speak. His face was beet red, and he was trying to keep from laughing out loud. On the top half of my body I looked like an 80-year old who just got home from playing Bridge with her friends. On the bottom half, I looked like one of Madonna's background dancers. "Uh huh, cute." That was all Marshall was able to get out before he started to laugh, his whole body shaking. He was trying to align himself with me so she couldn't see his face.

"Uh huh? Young man, your oratory skills...atrocious. I feel concerned for your future and, therefore, my granddaughter's as well. You might want to consider another line of work, because you'll never make it as an educator! NEVER! Regardless, Rachel, since this outfit looks so perfectly suited to your shape and coloring, I'd like to go ahead and give it to you because it doesn't fit me anymore. Would you like it?"

So a 78-year old woman passed down an outfit to her 19-year old granddaughter. That seems logical.

"Oh, yes, thank you, grandma" I said, knowing there was no other acceptable answer. "Thank you." I started to laugh again, covered my face and zipped away, trying to act like I was coughing which only caused me to expel an intestinal air bubble. That caused grandma to say, "What was that?" which only made me laugh harder!

I got behind my grandma and turned to see my mom and fiancé smiling at me. As I walked back into grandma's bedroom to change, I heard her ask Marshall if he thought that outfit looked nice on me. Once again, I shook with laughter as I heard him struggle to answer her with fake sincerity.

So that was my husband's introduction to this, now dead, grandmother. Again, not a huge loss. Perhaps you have a grouchy, mean, miserable grandparent, and you understand completely. Winifred Machock had a gift for making me feel terrible about myself. It wasn't personal though, she made *everyone* feel that way.

One of my cousins recently told me she would mail Winnie letters. Days later she'd get her letters back in the mail with red marks on all her grammatical errors. Grandma would correct the letter and return it to her, expecting her to rewrite the letter, fixing all the mistakes, then resend it.

I was so envious of my friends who actually liked their grandmothers. I longed for an older, godly grandmother who would teach me things, and love me unconditionally. Those qualities were absent from both of my grandmothers. Neither of them seemed to like me, let alone love me. I've always struggled with feeling rejected by women, in general. That feeling started with my own family. I tried to please the women in my family, but never felt like I succeeded. I tried to speak well so I could earn Grandma Winnie's respect. If I did have her respect, it was her well-kept secret.

Sometimes today when I'm speaking to someone, especially if they seem to be highly intelligent, I feel self-conscious. For so many years I felt inadequate because of Winifred. If I made the slightest mistake with my grammar, I felt foolish. The enemy used my grandmother's critical spirit to shame me.

There were a few things I liked about going to Winnie's house though. I loved those huge, beautiful Liquid Amber Maple trees in her front yard and the rich color of the Redwood planks that made up the exterior of her house. I also loved saying I had to go to the restroom, then sneaking off into her bedroom to look through her movie star-like jewelry box. I'd also take a quick peek into her closet and see these fur coats, and a turquoise, velvet pea coat and red patent leather shoes and a black velvet cocktail dress. I SOOOO wanted to play dress-up with them, but she'd never have it. The most I could do was look at them on these quick, fraudulent "trips to the restroom" when I had to "micturate."

Grandma was a Scrooge, no doubt. However, today as I write this and I think of her bitter spirit, I'm struck by another trait that marked her. When she spoke of her husband (who died before I was born), her speech was always brimming with adoration. It was practically the only time I heard her say something nice. She had the same kind of regard for her husband that I have for my own. It might be the *only* thing we had in common (well, that and the fact that peach and brown are in both of our color wheels).

When I look at my husband I feel enamored. As I'm writing this we've been married for 20 years, and I'm still so in love with him. He hung the moon, as far as I'm concerned. My grandma seemed to have the same feelings towards her late husband, my grandfather. The way she spoke of him was poetic, endearing, and just so sweet. It was the one and only time I ever saw an ounce of tenderness in her. Perhaps I too would be a bitter, angry crank if the love of my life left me at age 53, the way hers had. I don't know, and I don't want to find out.

My grandmother and I understand the power of a deep and abiding, love-filled, passionate marriage few ever know. She was blessed because she'd loved like that. I tried to have mercy on her grumpiness because she'd lost her love way too soon. So, perhaps we had several things in common: we were both very lucky in love, we both have had great highs and lows in our lives, and we both look great in peach and brown.

Winnie taught me how to speak proper English, and how to use impeccable manners. That's been a skill I've been thankful to have. In certain situations I've been relieved to know the proper way to communicate and handle myself. As annoying as her constant corrections were, I owe her for that.

I find some irony in the fact that it was this cantankerous grandmother with whom I never had a good relationship who would connect to me to the first person to notice and acknowledge my soul's pain. It was Grandma Winifred's priest who would skip straight to depth of what really mattered when my grandma would have never talked about such things. Even though I was nervous and reluctant to have Father John pray for me, his recognition of my depression did seize my curiosity. The yin and the yang.

So, Grandma Winnie was dead and Father John was coming over on February 10th. You win some and you lose some (Grandma's death, of course, being the 'win'). I calculated what day I should call and cancel with Father John. Should I do it sooner rather than later to get that weight off my shoulders? Should I call the morning of and say I'm sick? I rolled over my options. I knew that I'd figure something out. What I did not know was that my dark world was about to get rocked, and it would *never* be the same again.

Question: Is there someone in your life Satan has used to make you feel "less-than" in any way? Today as you think about that person, can you see their activity as a reflection of who they are instead of who you are? Can you see it as an attempt of Satan to shame you so you wouldn't have the confidence to be your best? Ask God to help you forgive that person. Talk to a counselor to help you remove the roots of shame that remain in your soul from that issue.

Another Question: Have you ever looked at a potential lifeline with disdain because of doubt, fear, or pride? Might you to need to re-examine an offer that's been given to you? I was so certain that Father John's offer was a waste of time. Have you ever looked at someone's offer to help you and assumed that it was not worthwhile?

Endnote:

[1] Indigo Girls. "Closer To Fine." Recorded 1989. Epic.

CHAPTER 9

Heavenly Lights

Everybody's got a cross to carry
Everybody's got a story they can tell
You know you're not the only one
Counting on a quarter and wishin' well
Don't you sit there with your heart under lock and key
Give me one chance, baby, I can set you free
When the sun is hard to find, when it's rainin' in your eyes
When the shadows block those pretty little blue skies living inside you
And when the fallin' of your tears, makes a candle disappear
When you just can't see the light, baby, I'll find a way to shine [1]

The morning of February 10th arrived as quickly as that high school exam you forgot about. I had determined the most compassionate lie I could tell Father John was that I was sick. So, early on the 10th I picked up the phone, dialed, and mentally prepared my "sick voice" for when he answered.

There was no answer.

I called again, and again, but no answer, no voicemail, no answering service, nothing.

I continued to call feverishly, starting to feel panicked that my plan might be backfiring.

Remember this was 1997. The phone number I had for him was for a landline, not a cell phone. In those days only a handful of rich people carried cell phones with them. Because he lived in Madera, I knew my chances of reaching him before he left to come to our house were dwindling.

It was now 12:30 and FINALLY-someone answered! Unfortunately, it was the church secretary, and she said he'd already left for Fresno to run some errands before meeting with us. She said she had no way of contacting him before he came to our home.

A wave of frustration and dread rolled over me as I considered the likelihood of this man actually showing up at our 450 square-foot apartment. My plan failed.   He *was* coming. I felt nervous in a way that defied logic. He's going to pray for me; I thought, why am I so anxious? But I felt nervous to the point of having a panic attack.

Marshall got home from work and was chipper and joyfully excited for Father John's arrival, which bugged me. I hadn't told him of my plan to cancel. The closer it got to 2:00, the harder my heart was beating.

When I heard the doorbell, I felt like I was going to throw up. I asked Marshall to get the door, and I headed to the bathroom. Through the paper thin walls I heard the baritone booming voice of Father John. He and Marshall were making small talk as I knelt before the white ceramic throne fearing my lunch was going to surface and be expelled. The only thing that scared me more than Father John praying for me was throwing up. I suffered from something called emetophobia; the fear of vomiting. So the only reasonable prayer I could pray at that point was "Lord Jesus, just as you turned water into wine, please turn this vomit into diarrhea."

Eventually I was back on my feet, heading down the one-and-a-half-foot path from the bathroom to the living room. I was sweaty and shaky and working to hide both. I was not sick, just afraid. I used to be sick a lot, but later realized that it was actually just sick thoughts making my body *feel* sick. Fear made me sick to my stomach often which was problematic in light of my emetophobia. The side effects of fear made me afraid. Fear also made my palms sweat and my heart race; it made me dizzy, gave me a headache, made me light-headed, gave me tunnel vision, and caused hearing problems. Did I mention that it made me feel like I was going to throw up? Good times.

So, I stepped out and put on my "nice enough face." I didn't necessarily want to make him feel overly welcomed.

"Well hello, Rachel." Father John's voice sounded like an earthquake rumbling. His six-foot, eight-inch frame towered over me.

"Hi." I said, but not with an abundance of warmth. Father John made me so nervous. No matter which face I put on, he seemed to know the truth. That terrified me...and fascinated me.

Marshall offered Father John some water and brought some for all of us, continuing to make small talk with our guest while I sat silently. I have no idea what they even talked about because all I could hear was the pounding sound of my heart in my head.

Marshall suggested that we sit at the dining room table. Marshall sat the head of the table, I was to his left, and Father John to his right.

Father John started by saying, "Sometimes when I pray for people they are healed from things. The other day when we were at the hospital I could see the pain in Rachel's eyes and thought God would like touch that pain." Marshall shook his head, but I sensed he was nervous, too. I wondered what "touch that pain," meant exactly, but before I could give it much thought I heard, "So, let's go ahead and just pray. Is that okay?"

Marshall and I looked at each other and shook our heads in agreement. Father John stood up and reached his gigantic arm across the table to anoint my forehead with oil in a cross formation and said, "In the Name of The Father, Son, and Holy Spirit…"

I'd never been anointed with oil (and didn't know it was in the Bible), so I chalked it up to some weird Episcopalian tradition and hoped the oil wouldn't cause any acne problems on my forehead. I wanted to wipe it off, but that seemed rude.

Father John sat down and began to pray what seemed to be a generic prayer:

"Dear Heavenly Father, we come to you on behalf of Rachel today…"

And I don't remember the rest. About two sentences into his prayer, I was "taken away." Those are the only words I can think of to describe what happened to me.

My eyes were closed as he prayed, then suddenly my eyes were opened and I was in the most glorious place I'd ever seen. It resembled a golden igloo, and it felt like I was in the center of the sun. The bright light was a beautiful golden tone with hints of amber and white.

I looked towards the entrance and saw angels coming in and going out, and I stared at them in awe. It was fascinating to watch their process. They were beautiful, glowing beings and seemed to be very clear on where they were to be at every given moment. One was coming in from an assignment as another was going out on assignment. They appeared to be moving in and out as if trying to get the right combination, for what I'm not certain.

My eyes shifted and I realized that as the angels came in, they were spreading their arms and taking their spots on the wall. As I looked closer, I realized that the walls were not walls. They were angels. The wall of angels was pulsating with their breath and the slightest movement of their wings, all moving in perfect unity.

I looked up and down in every direction and became conscious of the fact the entire structure was made up of angels. It was breathtaking, indescribable, and majestic.The beauty of it all captured my full attention.

Then I realized, if angels can come in and out, perhaps something dangerous could get in, too. At that instant, the entrance closed and was sealed with angels who were standing guard.

"WOW!" I just had the smallest THOUGHT that something dangerous could come in and immediately it was taken care of! Where am I and how powerful are my thoughts? I quickly understood that it was not the power of my thoughts, it was the power of The Light. The Light knew my thoughts, cared about my feelings, and made sure I was taken care of.

The intensity of that understanding is very complex, and I feel unable to articulate what it felt like. While in this place I understood things on a cellular level. There were no words being spoken, just messages inserted directly into my spirit. It was kind of like a dream where you just know things even though they aren't being explained to you.

At first it felt like God was in this sphere of golden light with me. Then it hit me: God is not *in* the ball of golden light with me. God *IS* the Light. I think of a Scripture I once heard, "God is Light; in Him there is *no darkness at all*" (1 John 1:5). He's not *near* the light nor *in* the light, He *IS* THE LIGHT. I floated, enjoying His brilliant presence. My spirit rested for the first time, *probably ever.*

As I stood, or rather floated, in The Light, the love of God became an overwhelming reality to me in a much deeper way than I'd ever experienced. I thought I'd understood His love from the time that His presence had settled in my room taking the form of a cloud when I was in Junior High. This was MUCH more potent. These words paraded through my mind:

> *Holy, Holy, Holy is the Lord God Almighty!*
> *Who was and Who is, and Who is to come!*
> *Holy, Holy, Holy is the Lord God Almighty!*
> *Who was and Who is, and Who is to come!*

I also had physical sensations as I rested there in this golden sphere. I could feel the warmth on my skin and I could feel the air around me, as if the molecules were larger here. They were large enough to *feel* the air. There is no earthly experience I can compare it to.

I perceived that the golden Light beams had healing power in them. It was like the beams contained health, joy, vitamins, peace, and the most quintessential Shalom that exists. I sat amidst the golden rays receiving radiation treatment for my cancer of the soul. The peace could not be compared to anything I've experienced before or since. I did NOT want to leave, but my spirit received a nudging from The Light. It was time to go. I didn't want to, and I considered throwing a tantrum like a two-year old to see if The Light would let me stay. But I decided against it.

I had to go back; they were waiting for me.

I was allowed to take in one last breath of this rare, thick, healing air, my skin to receive one last surge of healing warmth, and my spirit one last infusion of all things sublime.

Father John and Marshall were waiting. I'd already been there two or three minutes, and I couldn't keep them waiting any longer. So, with much reluctance, I returned and was shocked by what I found upon my re-entry to earth!

Question: Have you ever experienced God in a supernatural way? Would you be open to His moving in ways that are outside the box? Trust me, the best stuff is outside of the box!

Endnote:

1 Urban, Keith. "Shine." Recorded 2006. Capitol Records Nashville.

CHAPTER 10

I'm Back, Now What?

"The magical, supernatural force that is with us every second is time. We can't even comprehend it. It's such an illusion, it's such a strange thing." [1]

I was "back in my chair" and when I opened my eyes, I noticed the tablecloth in front of me was soaked. "Why is the table all wet?" I asked. Marshall leaned forward toward me, and he was white as a ghost.

"*Are you okay?*" he asked with terror in his voice.

That confused me because I was as high as a kite.

"Yes, I'm *wonderful*! I've never been better! What's wrong? Why is the table all wet? Did I spill my water?"

Marshall's voice was strained. "*Those are your tears*! You've been *SOBBING* for nearly two hours straight! ARE YOU *SURE*

YOU'RE OKAY?"

Sobbing? Sobbing for *two hours*? I was thoroughly confused. I had been "gone" for two minutes, not two hours. I was the happiest I'd EVER been, not *sobbing*! Nothing added up. Maybe Marshall was confused. I looked up at the clock and sure enough, *two hours had gone by*!

I had no previous experience with this and no way of understanding what was going on. Why the discrepancy in time? Why did I feel such joy when I'd been crying for two hours? And *why* was I crying? How did I not know that I'd been crying? This was bizarre.

I quit trying to figure it out and just continued to bask in the afterglow that I felt from my time with The Light. My mind drifted away from the table again and I just sat in euphoria. In the distant background, as if through a tunnel, I heard Father John explain to Marshall what was happening with me and hoped he continued to comfort him while I floated happily along.

My 'God-experiences' are difficult to explain, and they often deposit something into me that is confusing to others, because I can't quite describe it. It's intangible and unnamable, and incredibly wonderful, and that's frustrating to me because when something like this happens, I want those I love to get to feel it and fully understand it. But they don't. Some try, but they just can't.

The people who seem to understand this phenomenon are those who have had their own un-earthly experiences. On those rare occasions when we meet and for a moment exchange an understanding of one another's supernatural exploits in a deep-seated way, there is pure delight. Those are some of the sweetest moments of fellowship I've ever had. But that doesn't seem to happen very often. Perhaps more people have these types of supernatural experiences than it seems, but they fear being labeled as hyper-spiritual or weird, so they keep their experiences to themselves.

I am persuaded that those who step into the deep, those who seek God with all their hearts, and those who give all of themselves to this quest can have these types of experiences. Some of these encounters seem to be reserved for the broken-hearted, but certainly not all of them. If you long to taste of the amazing, unexplainable things of God, ask Him for that. Then, seek Him with all your heart.

> *You will seek me and find me when you seek me with all your heart.*
> *(Jeremiah 29:13, NIV)*

I heard Father John addressing me, so I reigned myself back in from the heights, trying hard to focus.

"I was just wondering if you could try to explain what you're feeling?" Father John asked.

"OK, sure." I paused and contemplated it all. How in the world do I explain what just happened to me? I couldn't fully grasp it myself. I explained what I saw and felt as best as I could, yet I felt frustrated by my inability to help them *feel* the wonder and awe of it.

Marshall was clearly struggling to process what I was saying. Father John looked like he'd heard all this so many times before. Then he asked about the sadness I'd been feeling and how I was feeling now. I stopped and took a second to really *feel* the joy, like nothing I'd ever experienced.

Marshall had a sense of relief as I spoke of the euphoria, and

Father John just shook his head and said, "Good. Well then, I'll be going now."

Just like that, his work was done.

Later I asked Father John to forgive me for my bad attitude towards him. He was as gracious as he could be and said he understood. It's amazing how I went from feeling so annoyed by him to feeling so indebted to him. To this day I thank God for Father John and others like him who can see past what we present ourselves to be and see the truth. Not only could Father John see I was depressed (even though I tried to look happy); he could also see past my annoyance with him to what my spirit was really longing for...to be healed.

Nothing Compares

My experience with The Light is so precious to me! I treasure the memory of all God did in me that day in my tiny little apartment with a man I didn't like very much. No one would ever be in The Light and voluntarily leave it. No matter how great your earthly experience, it fails miserably in every single way when compared to a heavenly one. That experience was a gift like none other!

As I write this now, I'm sitting in my beautiful home, in a comfortable chair next to an open window with a cool breeze coming through. A candle lit, my children are happy, quietly playing on the floor next to me, and I have a refreshing drink in my hand. As truly delightful as this circumstance is, it doesn't compare to the one I had that day. Nothing compares to being with The Light. I want to go back to The Light. I want to feel It's warmth again. It's a blessed, intoxicating experience.

After that day, I would never again be the same. I would encounter deep darkness again, but The Light that was infused into me that day would be with me through it all. That Light made the darkness bearable. I couldn't continue to live in the condition I was in prior to this event. Heaven, God, angels - they were no longer a belief. They were now empirically realized on a whole new level, and that was a game-changer for me. If not for that experience one cold February afternoon in 1997, I believe I'd be in an insane asylum or dead.

Later that night after Father John had left, I went to bed with my heart full of miraculous giddiness. My room smelled like wild honey as I drifted into a deep, sweet sleep (again, maybe for the first time). Then, I had a dream, a good one this time. In the dream I was back in the home I'd lived in from 3rd grade to 8th grade, the house I lived in when the pastor's advances began. In the dream I saw myself as a little girl. I was dressed in a beautiful, white dress, the kind of dress little girls want to wear, pretty, dainty, lacy, flowing down. I was dancing all around the living room of that childhood home.

The house was dark, but surrounding my sweet, little girl frame was a bright, intense "God light." I could tell The Light was the same Light I'd been with earlier that day, although in the dream it took the shape of a spotlight shining right on me. Darkness was lurking just beyond the edge of that spotlight, snarling at me. It took me back, but God quickly spoke to my fears.

"Sweet Rachel, notice that while the darkness is all around, wherever you go, so goes The Light."

I received the comfort God offered; in spite of darkness' presence in my life, The Light was always with me. As I danced around in my dream, delighting myself in the Lord, I stayed in this center of The Light. As I stayed in the center of The Light

I blossomed. The Light didn't make the darkness cease to exist, but it made me OKAY is spite of darkness' presence. I knew one day I might be required to look that darkness square in the eyes and go to battle with it. I filed that last bit of information into "things never spoken of."

The next morning when I awoke something was different. I was different. I saw my whole childhood in a different light. I had a calmness, believing that The Light had been with me every step of the way. There was a sense of well-being that was foreign and wonderful.

The first time I heard the song, "Priceless" by the group For King and Country, it felt like it was written about my dream.:

I see you dressed in white
Every wrong made right
I see a rose in bloom
At the sight of you
Oh, so priceless
Irreplaceable, unmistakable, incomparable
Darling, it's beautiful
I see it all in you
Oh, so priceless
No matter what you've heard,
This is what you're worth
More than all the money or the diamonds and pearls
Oh, this is who you are
Yeah, this is who you are
So when it's late,
You're wide awake
Too much to take
Don't you dare forget
That in the pain
You can be brave,
Hear me say
I see you dressed in white
Every wrong made right

I see a rose in bloom
At the sight of you
Oh, so priceless
Irreplaceable, unmistakable, incomparable
Darling, it's beautiful
I see it all in you
Oh, so priceless
Sisters, we can start again
Give honor 'til the end
Love, we can start again [2]

I had that dream of me dressed in white in 1997. Twenty years later I heard For King and Country's song, "Priceless". It was as if the writers were observers in my dream and then wrote a song to describe what they saw. In 2017 I had the honor of hosting For King and Country while they were in town to perform. It was a joy to look them in their eyes and tell them what their song meant to me. Another wild honey moment for sure!

Luke Smallbone, Me, and Joel Smallbone

The trauma that marked my first 20 years of life would have

taken my life had God Himself not infused me with Himself, the purest Light of all. He made me "good enough" that day, and it would be 17 years before I would transition from good enough to a deeper, richer, fuller form of freedom and healing. This kind of freedom would require me to confront the demons of those first 20 years, the darkness in my dream. Confronting demons requires a great amount of courage. God would use two more dreams to get me to take the courage He offered me. It was time. You could say it was "for such a time as this."

Endnotes:

1 Hopkins, Anthony. Access April 1, 2017. https://www.brainyquote.com/quotes/keywords/every_second.html

2 Luke Smallbone, Joel Smallbone, Mosley, Seth, Tedd Andrew Tjorhom, and Benjamin Backus. "Priceless." Recorded 2016. Fervent/Curb.

CHAPTER 11

I Like Him

Goodnight, my angel
Time to close your eyes
And save these questions for another day
I think I know what you've been asking me
I think you know what I've been trying to say
I promised I would never leave you
And you should always know
Wherever you may go
No matter where you are
I never will be far away [1]

Make It Stop

"How many days have you been bleeding at this point?" the stunning, Irish nurse practitioner asked me.

"54"

"Yikes, 54. okay. We're going to do some investigating here. Something's not right...*obviously*. I'd like to do some blood work and do an examination. Don't worry, sweetheart, we're going to take care of this. You're going to be fine."

I really didn't want to do an examination, but I also didn't want to bleed for a 55th day. She slipped out, and I slipped on the loveliest little hospital gown you've ever seen. I was 20 years old and had only had a couple of these types of examinations at this point. The whole idea of it made me feel like I was going to throw up. But, I was even more afraid of throwing up than I was of this type of exam, so I took some deep breaths and swallowed hard.

The beautiful, emerald eyed, red haired, freckled nurse practitioner stepped back into the room and asked if I was ready. That always feels like a dumb question to me. No, I'm not ready. I'll never be ready. What came out of mouth was "Yes."

I laid down on the cold, hard, paper covered exam table and prayed. The nurse was gentle and kind and funny. At that moment I appreciated all three of those qualities. She finished my exam, rolled off her latex gloves, stood up and came up to my side, sweetly resting her hand on top of my mine. She looked into my eyes with a deep sense of compassion and said, "Honey, have you ever been abused?"

"No!" I quickly answered. She looked at me with a look that said, "I know you're lying. You're safe here. You can tell me. My heart hurts for you. Please let me help you."

Even though I'd answered her question, she sat looking at me waiting for a different answer, but I wasn't about to tell her anything. I just sat looking at her and thinking I will win this stare down because I'm not talking. In a way, I'd also never thought about the things that happened to me as being abuse. I know that sounds weird, but I think I needed to make my life's events more palatable to myself so I'd reframed them.

I thought of what I'd been through as a series of unfortunate events that happened, just like everyone has unfortunate things that have happened to them. I literally didn't think the heinous things I'd experienced were much different than what anyone else had been through. I just thought I didn't handle my unfortunate things as well as most people handled theirs. So when she asked me if I'd been abused, on one hand I wanted to tell her some things that had happened that *might* be contributing to my bleeding for 54 days straight. On the other hand, I didn't put my experiences in the abuse column. We often lie to ourselves when our truth is too painful.

After a long silent pause, her eyes brimmed with tears, and she said, "Okay, sweetheart. Okay," as she patted my hands with so much tenderness. It makes me cry thinking about it. She was so eager to help me. But I wasn't ready to be helped. Maybe you've tried to help someone you know needed help, but she wouldn't receive your help. Just know sometimes people can't be helped.... *yet.* Sometimes they just can't handle it...*yet.*

She blotted her eyes, and her crying annoyed me. Now I understand her crying caused me to feel the pain I was constantly trying to avoid. Her acknowledging that something was not right with my body caused me so much discomfort, even though she was being sweet. I didn't want to think about difficult things. I just wanted her to make the bleeding stop and let me go home.

She sat down and asked me to sit up. She said, "This might be a difficult thing to hear, but I need to tell you something. When you decide to have kids, that might not happen for you. I know you just got married, and you're so young, so you're probably not ready now anyway. When you are ready though, you will need to plan on receiving the help of a fertility specialist. Here at Kaiser you have to be trying to get pregnant for a minimum of one year before you can get help from a specialist. However, because of some special circumstances here, I am going to have that waiting period waved for you. Since we can already determine your likelihood of conceiving will be very low, you won't have to wait a year. Okay, honey?"

I didn't have the first clue why she was saying this. I assumed it was because of the bleeding. That was part of it. However, I now realize she was saying that based on what she saw during my physical exam. We hadn't even done blood work yet, and she was saying, "You're probably not going to be able to conceive." She was telling me this because of the evidence she'd just witnessed.

This was completely devastating to me. When I was little, I wanted to be so many things, but the main role I longed for was that of a mom. When I got home later that day I told my sweet husband about what she'd said, and we talked about how we would adopt if we couldn't have kids ourselves. I went into denial or faith, depending on how you look at it. I bounced back from being disappointed, and I really didn't believe the nurse. I believed somehow, someway, I would have kids.

Baby? What baby?

A few weeks after that examination, I was lying in bed early in the morning. Marshall left early for school. He was taking 18 units, and working many hours a week at a law firm. I was also going to school full time and waitressing.

This morning I was flat on my back, staring at our apartment ceiling, when suddenly my radio popped on. It scared me because I'd already turned off my alarm. I looked over to turn it off, and the nob was turned to "OFF," but it was "ON."

I tried to turn it off, but no matter what I did, I couldn't figure it out. Then, I became mesmerized by what was on the radio. It was talk radio with Charles Stanley speaking with that beautiful Georgia drawl. One of his sermons was being broadcast. I slowly laid back down and began listening to him. He was telling the story of Hannah, the barren woman who was distraught.

I'd heard the story before, but now I was hearing it with the ears of a barren woman. As he moved through the story, I felt a sense of excitement rise up in me. I could tell the Lord had arranged for me to hear this sermon at that very moment and He'd caused my radio to defy its "OFF" status.

At the end of the sermon I heard the Lord say into my spirit, "You too will have a son, and he too will belong to me. Your firstborn will be a boy, and you will raise him up, teaching him My ways, and then you will give him back to Me. Just like Hannah gave Samuel back to me, you will give Jackson back to Me." Marshall and I had already determined our first son would be named Jackson. My spirit leapt. I knew I *was* going to be able to have kids after all! I got out of bed with a strong sense I was not barren; or if I was, the Lord planned to heal me.

What I didn't know that morning was that I was already pregnant.

Marshall and I had been married for 10 months; we were still poor college students. I was still waitressing. He was working as a court runner, running documents from a law firm down to the courthouse. We made less than $13,000 a year with both of our incomes *combined*. You could say it was not an ideal time to get pregnant, but God's ways are certainly not our ways. Even though the timing was not ideal, we were thrilled to be having a baby!

The Circle of Life

My pregnancy was fine. Things had gone smoothly. I was waitressing all through the pregnancy, which was hard, but I managed. I was young, and I loved the feeling of a life growing inside me. I loved feeling my baby move. Marshall and I were so excited to become parents.

Around the 34th week of the pregnancy, I developed a very bad headache. I'd had migraine headaches my whole life, so I didn't think anything of it. I just tried to press through and tough it out, but it kept getting worse. It felt like my head was going to explode.

Thinking it was a migraine and that my only option was to grin and bear it, I did just that until I was going on 48 hours of no sleep. The pain in my head was so intense I hadn't been able to relax enough to sleep. So, I concluded I needed to go to the hospital for an injection of pain medicine.

We arrived at Kaiser and they took a urine sample and my blood pressure. My urine was loaded with protein, and my blood pressure was so high they expected I would soon have a stroke and even seizures, so they admitted me. They began pumping my body with magnesium to lower my blood pressure. Magnesium has many effects. It made me lose my vision and throw up. It was a terrifying time. I was delusional from having not slept for so long, was throwing up (one of my worst fears), had lost my vision, and I was so scared.

They informed me I had something called Pre-eclampsia, and

they were going to have me deliver the baby, as that was the only way to save my life. They gave me medicine to induce labor, which caused more pain, but no real progress. When my water finally broke, we called the nurse. She came into the room, excited to hear of my progress. She pulled back the blankets to examine me, but froze, then yelled for another nurse.

There was frantic activity around me. The door was flying open and shut as person after person flew into my room. One sweet nurse came up to my head, stroked my hair and said, "Honey, everything is going to be okay. But your water did not break. You're hemorrhaging. We're going to be taking you in for a C-section now. Everything is going to be okay." I tried to believe her, but I couldn't help but wonder why her voice was quivering.

Before I could process what was happening, I was being rushed down the hallway on a gurney. The anesthesiologist came running in to the operating room, yelling and demanding that my stats be given to him. I asked where Marshall was. I wanted him with me. That same sweet nurse was still standing at my head stroking my hair, but now she was full on crying. She leaned over my head and as her tears fell onto my face she said, "You're doing great!" I wondered why she was crying if I was doing so great. Then I heard the anesthesiologist say, "We're losing mom. I'm switching to saving baby."

He inserted into my body a general block, meaning he numbed my entire body so they could cut into me immediately. This paralyzed my lungs and I stopped breathing. I tried to scream for help to tell them I couldn't breathe, but discovered when you can't breathe you can't speak either. They shoved an intubation tube down my throat just as I was losing consciousness.

He's Nice!

The next thing I know I'm in a calm, quiet place and I hear the sweetest voice. There was a male nurse with a beard standing next to my bed. He was talking to me and telling me I was going to be okay. It was just the two of us in the room. He told me Jackson was going to be okay too. I asked him questions, mostly about Jackson – what he looked like and how much he weighed. He answered all my questions and tended to me, physically and emotionally. I liked him *a lot*. He had such a warm spirit, and he was incredibly reassuring. As we spoke, I knew all was well with me and with Jackson, and my spirit was infused with peace...*again*.

A few days later I was finally becoming less groggy. My body was not healing the way it should, but for the most part I didn't worry about that. I was happy to have Jackson. He was so tiny, so pure, so precious. I thought about him being the fulfillment of what God had spoken to me that morning while I laid in bed listening to Charles Stanley. I didn't really know how to "give him back to God," but knew I'd figure it out. I was so young and so confused. I wanted to be a good mom worse than anything and found that sheer determination, commitment, and a lot of prayer will take you far, no matter how confused you are.

After I began getting my vision back, I asked my nurse if she would please track down that male nurse that had stayed with me in the hours following Jackson's birth. I told her I really wanted to thank him. He'd helped me so much! She said she'd go find out when he would be working next and bring him to my room.

Later she slipped back in and said, "I've looked at your chart for the entire time you've been here, and you've never had a male nurse. None of the people that cared for you during that time were male, except the doctor and the anesthesiologist. Was it one of them?"

I knew who they were, and the man I was talking about was not either of them. I asked her to recheck because I really wanted to spend more time with him and, at the very least, I wanted to thank him.

She re-checked and there had not been a man with me. I was puzzled and thought through what he looked like, how sweetly he'd spoken to me, and about our conversation. I told my nurse all about it and she said, "You were intubated, unconscious, and unable to speak during the timeframe you're saying you had this conversation with this man." I also realized the medicine I was taking at that time caused me to lose my vision, yet I could see him with perfect clarity. My hospital room began having the aroma of wild honey.

In an instant it hit me, that was *not* a nurse. Was it Jesus? Was it an angel? No wonder I liked him so much! No wonder he was incredibly warm and kind. No wonder I was infused with peace as he spoke. *No* wonder...yet...*total* wonder!

Yet another glimpse into the euphoria that comes from heaven. Right in the middle of the trauma, the fear, the breathlessness, the hemorrhaging, heaven emerges. The Light makes itself known again. It is in the middle of the darkest darkness we can experience brightest Light. For those who love Him...

Question: Have you ever interacted with an angel? The Bible says we will entertain angels and be unaware of it (Hebrews 13:11). I'm one that wants to be aware. I ask God this all the time: God, will you please help me to *see* Your activity around me. Help me not to miss a thing! I want to have my eyes opened to what You're doing, to who You're sending onto my path, and

I don't want to miss You! I want to experience EVERYTHING that YOU want me to experience.

God gives me what I've asked for. I see Him and His activity all around me, all the time. And all I did was ask to see. For those who love Him, He will do MORE than we can ask or imagine (Ephesians 3:20)! Ask!

Endnote:

1 Joel, Billy. "Lullabye (Goodnight, My Angel)." Recorded 1994. Columbia Records.

CHAPTER 12

Medicate Me, Please

Another Emergency Miracle

Two years and nine months after Jackson was born, Jonah Thomas Hamm entered the world. He had jet black hair and olive skin. He was beautiful, as was the process of birthing him.

After the trauma of Jackson's birth I had substantial amounts of anxiety about delivering again. Thankfully, Jonah's birth was peaceful, healthy, and joyful. The stress that accompanied Jackson's birth wasn't present for his. Jonah's birth felt redemptive and it brought me much-needed healing.

Jonah was an easy going, low maintenance baby. Jackson's first time to sleep through the night was on his first Birthday. Jonah started sleeping through the night when he was just six-weeks old. Jackson had a lot of trouble with eating and struggled to gain weight. Jonah ate like it was going out of style. He was chubby, happy, and adorable. Jonah's laid back demeanor helped me enjoy life and motherhood so much.

Jonah continues to make me smile as he is deep-thinking, witty, charming, insightful, handsome, and discerning. He's quiet, until he's not. When he's "not" he can make me laugh harder than just about anyone can. He's always observing and noticing things that just fly right past my racing brain. I love his observations. They fascinate me.

Marshall and I went on to have another son just 19 months after Jonah was born. His name is Ethan and he's kind, honorable, creative, and precious. I love how each child brings something different to the table. Each one has a specific set of gifts and talents and a unique personality that enriches our family life. When I look at my sons I marvel at God's creativity.

I did NOT need fertility treatments to get pregnant with any of the boys. That fact is a constant reminder to me that God can do what He wants, when He wants, and how He wants. He'd healed my body from the abuse and, against all odds, had given me three precious sons.

I was so grateful I'd been able to have these fun boys, but I was struggling emotionally. I kept having panic attacks and had reached a point where I couldn't live like that anymore. I was still not acknowledging my abuse history. I was just trying to figure out how to "get through" life and move on. I was having to fight just to keep my head above water, and I was dog tired from dog paddling through life. Something had to change.

Early one evening I had taken a medicine I'd never taken before. After about an hour, I found myself having a hard time breathing, struggling to swallow; it felt like my throat was closing, like I was going to throw up. I was so dizzy I couldn't stand up, my body was shaking, and I felt like I had needles poking all over. Ironically, I was taking the medicine to help calm my body because I was caught in an intense stronghold of fear that was causing panic attacks.

This was the second time that I'd had an allergic reaction to an anti-anxiety medicine, but it was even more terrifying than the first! My husband had called 9-1-1 so now I was laying on my bed surrounded by four paramedics, three firemen, the fire chief, a couple police officers, and my husband. As I looked at all these men standing around my bed, all looking at me, my heart was full of fear and humiliation. What was happening to me? Was I going to live through this? Would my children be left motherless? I was struggling to breathe and attempting to keep my body still as I was having tremors I couldn't control.

Two of the paramedics were "working on me," checking all my vitals, and giving me oxygen. There was a third paramedic that had a strange look in his eye. He moved from the foot of my bed over to my nightstand. Even in my frantic physical state, I'd noticed that there was something different about this paramedic. As he approached my nightstand, he picked up my Bible, opened it (without asking), and in front of all these men confidently started declaring this over me:

"God is our refuge and strength,
an ever-present help in trouble.
Therefore we will not fear, though the earth give way and the
mountains fall into the heart of the sea, though its waters roar
and foam and the mountains quake with their surging.
There is a river whose streams make glad the city of God,
the holy place where the Most High dwells.
God is within her, she will not fall;
God will help her at the break of day.
Nations are in uproar, kingdoms fall; He lifts his voice, the earth

> *melts.*
> *The LORD Almighty is with us;*
> *the God of Jacob is our fortress.*
> *Come and see the works of the LORD,*
> *the desolations he has brought on the earth.*
> *He makes wars cease to the ends of the earth;*
> *he breaks the bow and shatters the spear,*
> *he burns the shields with fire.*
> *Be still, and know that I am God;..."*

That's when it happened. That's when God's Word took authority over my body and mind. When the paramedic read the words "BE STILL AND KNOW THAT I AM GOD," my tremors stopped, I felt like I could breathe normally, and the soundness of my mind returned. The loud fearful thoughts were silenced.

The paramedic continued,

> *"I will be exalted among the nations, I will be exalted in the earth.*
> *The LORD Almighty is with us; the God of Jacob is our fortress."* [1]

I looked at that paramedic and asked, "Are you a chaplain or pastor or something?" He laughed and responded, "No, I'm just a Christian who understands the power of God's Word." Whoa. Suddenly the taste of wild honey was on my tongue.

The Bible is Boring

That night was one in a series of unusual events where the Lord directed my attention to the power of His Word. He showed me in some bizarre ways that His Word was the answer to the problem, the solution I'd been searching for, the wisdom I needed, the purpose-giving power and peace that I'd longed for. His

Word did what anti-anxiety medicine had failed to.

That experience made me long to study Scripture for myself. I came to be a student of God's Word out of desperation. I'd love to say I just wanted to study God's Word, but I didn't. Before this experience with the bold paramedic I found God's Word to be a bit boring. When I read it, I usually started yawning, wanting a nap. I wasn't much of a reader anyway, and I especially didn't like reading something that didn't seem to be practical. I didn't always understand what I read in the Bible, and I certainly didn't see how it benefited my day-to-day life. So I rarely read it.

It wasn't until life was flat out not working that I ended up seeking help from God in His Word. It wasn't until my issues became bigger than I could handle. I was having multiple health issues that all led me to God's Word. Well, that's not exactly true. I was having health issues that led me to people who led me to God's Word. The first one was the paramedic.

Thank you For Your Courage!

That paramedic, who was a total stranger, directed me to God's Word as an answer to my anxiety issues. I've often thought about the amazing courage that man had! I wonder how hard it was for him to do that in that moment in front of all those men, one of whom was the fire chief of our city. Why were all those men there that night? After he told me he was just a man who understood the power of God's Word, he went on to explain he wasn't even a paramedic. He said he was just doing a ride along that night. Where did that man's courage come from? What if he'd felt moved to do that, but shrunk back out of embarrassment?

I know there have been times when I felt moved to do something, but didn't because I felt stupid. I'm sure it took a lot of courage for him to do that! How did his actions affect those other men that night? They ALL saw how my body and mind completely change as he declared God's Word over me. That was life changing for me. Thank God that man was so brave!

Issues of The Heart

Around the same time I'd tried that anti-anxiety medicine, I was having a stress test done with a cardiologist because of heart palpitations. We were pretty sure that anxiety was causing this problem, but my doctor wanted to rule out any heart issues, as they run in my family.

At first there was a nurse with me when I went for the test; and in then walked the cardiologist. He was a very tall, handsome, African-American man with a beautiful South-African/British accent. He wore glasses and a warm smile. At the end of the stress test, he said, "Okay, please stop. Have a seat." He pulled a chair over and sat down right in front of me and held out his huge hands to me, palms up. I put my hands into his giant hands. He folded his fingers over my hands, completely covering my hands with his. His eyes looked deep into my eyes and he said, "Do you have a relationship with Jesus Christ?"

Wait, what?

Stunned that this stranger would be asking me this, I responded, "Yes, I do."

"Good. Because there's nothing wrong with your heart, at least not your physical one. I think a stronghold of fear is caus-

154

ing your heart to feel jumpy. You should get to know your God better through His Word, and these "heart issues" would be probably clear right up." He said this to me with so much love and compassion. This doctor had the Holy Spirit oozing from his pores. He was a gentle giant. The love of the Father came through his eyes and in every word he spoke. That was the second time someone from the medical community showed me that what I needed wasn't going to be found in medicine, but in God's Word.

The third time was when I went to have an eye examination, and I had a panic attack during the exam. The doctor stopped the exam and asked me why I was afraid. Then he asked me if I was a Christian. When I said "yes," he said, "Then you need to study your Bible more because it clearly tells you God has not given you this spirit of fear. He's given you a spirit of power and of love, and of a SOUND MIND! If you're a believer, you're not to be afraid of *anything!*" [2]

He kind of bugged me, honestly. He was *not* sweet like the cardiologist and paramedic had been. He was very pushy about it. He questioned whether I had an authentic walk with the Lord since I was so bound by fear. He questioned how well I knew this God I'd supposedly entrusted my life to. I was ticked at how rude he was, but he made me think! I wonder if he was harsh because I'd not gotten the point with the first two messengers God sent me.

How sweet is God to lead us to answers when we seek Him. He's told us that we WILL find Him when we seek Him with all our hearts. [3]

God showed me that knowing Him through His Word was the answer I was looking for. I didn't need medicine. I didn't need a medical doctor. I needed to get to know my God, and find my healing directly from The Healer Himself.

At times that revelation was frustrating because medicine was a quick fix. Getting to know God and going through the *process* of renewing my mind with His Word would take a lot of time. I had to resist the temptation to get relief immediately in order to find true healing. Anti-anxiety medicine would have only been a band-aid for me. Renewing my mind, and dealing with the root of my issues brought true healing. The difference is night and day.

The process of renewing my mind caused my wounds to be cleaned, tended to, and healed instead of masking them with medicine. I had broken thoughts. God's Word replaced my broken thoughts with the life-giving truth. You shall know the truth, and the truth shall set you free.4 Anti-anxiety medicine gave me a false sense of security. My wounds were still festering, but anti-anxiety medicine just caused me not to care anymore. For the most part anti-anxiety medicine is a numbing agent.

If you're on anti-anxiety or anti-depressant meds right now, and my testimony is bothering you, talk to God about it. The Holy Spirit says He will lead us into all truth.[5] So, ask Him to do that for you. Ask Him if this applies to you. Ask Him to speak louder than your medicine, because when I was on those meds I could not hear the voice of the Lord. I was numb to pain, passion, and the voice of my God.

So, at that point in my life I couldn't deny God was leading me to His Word. That pesky ophthalmologist lit a fire under me. I really didn't like him, but I knew he had some legitimate questions for me, and I didn't have good answers for him.

Lord, Help Me....I'm BORED!

I wanted to do what I felt like God was showing me to do, but (as I said) I didn't like reading the Bible. That was a problem. I decided to come to the Lord and tell him I *wanted* to like reading His Word, but currently I didn't. I asked Him to help me actually like His Word. I also asked Him to help me understand what I read. I knew the Holy Spirit is our teacher, so before I read the Word, I asked the Spirit to instruct me as I read. Then, I asked the Lord to show me how His Word was relevant TO ME RIGHT WHERE I WAS. And you know what? HE DID! He did all I asked.

He also showed me some stumbling blocks I needed to deal with.

Once when I was studying, I looked up and said to Him, "This isn't working!" I was frustrated by the discrepancy between what I was reading and what I was experiencing. He quickly spoke right back and said, "WELL, OF COURSE IT ISN'T WORKING! YOU'RE READING MY WORD, BUT YOU'RE NOT *BELIEVING* MY WORD. YOU HAVE TO BELIEVE THAT IT'S THE TRUTH FOR IT TO 'WORK.'"

He showed me I could *choose* to believe it. I thought I needed to *feel* like it was true, but He showed me it was a CHOICE to believe the Bible was the true, divinely inspired, Word of God. So in that moment I chose to believe. That was a turning point for me.

Now, faith comes easy to me. When I feel like God speaks something into my spirit, it's easy for me to believe it quickly. I am not one who has had lots of doubts about God. Maybe that's because I've seen so many amazing miracles. Or maybe I've seen so many miracles because I have faith. I don't know if the chicken or the egg came first. I don't know why it's easy for me, but it is. Maybe I have the gift of faith. If you have lots of doubts, ask Him to lead you to the truth. You can always be honest with God about the struggles in your heart. He knows them all anyway.

After I made the choice to believe God and His Word, I became a sold-out lover of both! At this point I can say God's Word has completely renewed my mind. We're all a work in progress, but God's Word has truly transformed my thought life. It's torn down those strongholds of fear and replaced them with peace, joy, power, love, and a sound mind. That's what I call a miracle.

Perhaps you had to live inside my brain to know how bad it was in there to grasp the miraculous nature of what's taken place in me. Trust me when I say I am a new creation, and it is all because of God's Word.

I see my brain as a room with wallpaper on the walls. The wallpaper was fearful thoughts. God's Word was like a wallpaper remover. It stripped down all the fearful wallpaper and replaced it with new, clean walls.

So what does it mean to study God's Word? If you hated school and studying like I did, the word "study" might make you break out in a cold sweat. Despite the less than exciting associations most people have, studying God's Word can actually be one the most energizing, freeing, and exciting experiences we can have. Some of the best "highs" I've ever had were while studying Scripture.

The Reasons Why

Here are a few reasons I love to study God's Word:

1. Being in God's Word daily as a part of my disciplined life helps me more easily recognize a lie when I hear one.

We are living in age of deception, and as believers we MUST know the truth so we won't be deceived. The right way is not always obvious, and there are lying spirits eager to mislead us. Jesus warned us about that. The lying spirits don't just tell us outright lies; they mix a good dose of truth with a little bit of lie so it can be hard to detect. Reading God's Word daily helps us spot that kind of deception quickly.

2. I want to know what my rights are as a child of God, and I want to exercise them! If Christ came that I might have and enjoy life and have it in abundance, to the full, until it overflows, then I want to *know* that and I want to *have* that life, don't you? We are told in John 10:10 (AMP) that's one of the reasons Christ came. He also told us there is a thief that comes to steal, kill, and destroy us. God's Word gives us the wisdom we need to receive that abundant life from Christ and to know how to protect ourselves from that thief. We've got to be wise men and women of God to know *how* to do that. We become wise as we study God's Word. We have to walk in *Spirit* and in *truth*. Both are essential.

> *"Hear instruction and be wise, and do not refuse or neglect it. Blessed (happy, fortunate, to be envied) is the man who listens to me, watching daily at my gates, waiting at the posts of my doors. For whoever finds me (Wisdom) finds life and draws forth and obtains favor from the Lord. But he who misses me or sins against me wrongs and injures himself; all who hate me love and court death."*
> *(Proverbs 8:33-36, AMP)*

This Scripture implies we are either growing in our wisdom and knowledge of the Lord, or we are dying! We are "courting death."

We Don't Know What We Don't Know

Recently, I dealt with a very large company about a legal matter. They told me what I could and couldn't do in a certain situation. A friend of mine who knew the law knew that what this company told me wasn't true. So with his help I called the company on their lies. I told the man who'd helped me learn the law that I was shocked a company of this size and stature in the world would purposely lie to me. My friend said, "I'm not surprised. It would have worked out very nicely for them if you just wouldn't have known the truth, and most people don't know the truth so they get away with this all the time."

That's exactly what Satan is doing to the Christian community right now. He's getting away with a lot of lies because we don't know the truth well enough to recognize his lies when we hear them. If Satan can keep us from knowing what we have a right to, then he's successfully stolen the abundant life Christ came to give us. If Satan can keep us from being in God's Word, learning how to handle His Word, and how to apply it to our lives, he can render us ineffective for the Kingdom. God's Word is our double-edged sword. It's not just another book. It holds the keys to life and liberty.

Whey my boys were little, I'd tell them the Bible is the filter through which we take everything else in. Never let something in without screening it through God's Word. Does this line up with God's Word? Is this concept consistent with what we read in Scripture? Is this something that's consistent with the character of God based on what we already KNOW through Scripture? Knowing God through His Word becomes our protection. We are to guard our hearts and minds through Christ Jesus. We do this by knowing the Word.

Once I was in counseling with a good, Christian counselor, but he told me something that didn't line up with God's Word. If I were not a student of God's Word, I probably would have taken his advice and that would not have led me to God's best. We must know God's Word *for ourselves* and not be relying on ministers, counselors, pastors, our parents, or anyone else to tell us all we need to know. We ought to be able to listen to a pastor teach and know if what he is saying accurately lines up with God's Word. No one else's study of God's Word should replace our own study.

Submitting to God and God's Word will lead us to our fullest life. Every other path leads to death, even if we perceive it as life. There's no middle ground. Perhaps you think that I'm being too extreme with that statement. Remember what Jesus told us about being lukewarm? He said he'd "spit you out."

> *"I know your deeds, that you are neither cold nor hot. I wish you were one or the other! So, because you are lukewarm — neither hot nor cold — I am about to spit you out of my mouth."*
> *(Revelation 3:15-16, NIV)*

Or, as the genius Bob Dylan so aptly wrote,

> *You're going to have to serve somebody.*
> *It may be the devil, or it may be the Lord,*
> *but you're going to have to serve somebody.* [6]

God's Word must become the spiritual core from which all our desires, motivations, and decisions arise. Through study we exchange destructive habits for new, life-giving ways of thinking and living. I renew my mind with God's Word every day. Well, almost every day. The days I miss my time in the Word, I notice it. I feel like I'm a little off center. I notice a difference in my attitude, and my emotions when I miss my time in the Word.

Many years ago when I used to struggle with panic attacks, I took old fearful, faithless thoughts and replaced them with the truth of God's Word. I no longer have panic attacks. I am no longer dominated by fear the way I used to be. God's Word revolutionized my thinking.

We also need to know the "good news" that God freely gives grace to us through Christ. We study Scripture to know the heart and will of God. The central purpose of Scripture study is not simply to obtain religious information, but rather for *inner transformation*.

> *"All Scripture is God-breathed and is useful for teaching, rebuking, correcting and training in righteousness, so that the man (or woman) of God may be thoroughly equipped for every good work."*
> *(2 Timothy 3:16-17, NIV)*

When we study, we also learn how to have a healthy, humble perspective on ourselves and others. Studying God's Word not only shows us who God is; it shows us who we are. Studying God's Word gives us a filter with which we can view world events. This hurting world needs to know if our Jesus is still relevant to them today. They need to know that God's Word can transform their lives. Maybe *you* need to know that, too.

There will always be many excuses to keep us from studying. "I don't have the time" would probably be at the top of the list. I heard an older woman telling a younger mom she didn't need to worry about studying God's Word right now; she'd have time for that when her kids were grown. Nothing could be further from the truth! I understand this woman was trying to relieve the young mom from self-condemnation, but I don't think I ever needed God's Word quite as much as I did when all my boys were little. Not to mention, it would have been tough to be filling their little minds with God's Word if I wasn't first filling my own. We can't pass on what we don't have.

Other excuses we come up with are, "I don't know how to study. I don't like to read, or I don't understand what I read." I had some of these same excuses at one point, and I took them to the Lord, confessed how I was feeling, and simply asked for His help in these areas. When we seek help with sincere hearts, answers appear. We find what we are looking for. It's only when we don't look that we don't find.

OK, But HOW?

Perhaps you're wondering where to start? First, we start with a *decision* to make studying Scripture a priority. Second, we carve out time each day for our study time, then we guard that time fiercely. Nothing should sneak in and take away from our study time.

I made early mornings my study time and when one of my sons was about four years old, he started getting up whenever I got up. It didn't seem to matter what time I got up, he got up, too. So, in an effort to guard my study time, I told him if he was going to get up that early, he had to sit by me on the couch without talking, and with no TV, until my study time was over. It was a very frustrating time. It was hard to study with him right there sucking his thumb staring at me. And it took a lot of time to train him that I meant business. This was my time with God, and he needed to honor that.

Maybe you would have a more effective study time at night. There is no wrong time. I'm a morning person and my mind was mush once the sun went down.

3. Choose how you will study. Should you stick just to the Word and read directly from it alone? Should you pick a Bible study, or join a group that's doing a study? You may want to ask someone whom you respect what study aids she has used and would recommend to you. I've done a variety of things. Beth Moore's Bible studies (from Lifeway Publishing) have had a huge influence in my life as they have in so many other women's lives. I also love just reading straight from the Word and going through one book of the Bible at a time. When I switched to reading out of the Amplified Bible, I enjoyed Scripture more.

4. Find the right place for your study time. It needs to be comfortable, but not too comfortable. You might want to have a notebook, pens, a concordance, devotional books, or Bible study books and, of course, your Bible.

When I first began to study God's Word consistently, I used Bible study books and aids. I had a hard time studying Scripture by itself. For me, that was a great place to start. It got me into the Word and it gave me some much-needed guidance. Now, I prefer to study straight from the Scriptures.[7]

As I read, I think of it as a conversation between God and me. Often I will stop and speak back to God regarding what He just spoke to me through His Word. For example, I'm reading through Proverbs right now. So I'll read a passage like Proverbs 8:13 (NIV):

> "To fear the Lord is to hate evil;
> I hate pride and arrogance, evil behavior and perverse speech.
> Counsel and sound judgment are mine; I have understanding
> and power."

Then I'll stop and speak back to the Lord:

> "Lord, I want to love what You love and hate what You hate, so
> help me to hate pride and arrogance, evil behavior, and perverse

speech. And Lord, if there is any of that in me, help me to see that so I could have the opportunity to repent and turn from it. And Lord, as a mother, I desperately need Your godly counsel, sound judgment, and supernatural understanding. Seeing as how You have all these things, Lord, I ask that You would give them to me! I ask for these things, in Jesus' Name!"

Then, I would move on in my reading.

I also keep a concordance and Greek and Hebrew dictionary, which help me to have a deeper understanding of what the original text might have meant. I usually read one chapter each morning. Sometimes I read the same chapter in a different translation. Then, I take key words that jumped off the page and look them up in the dictionary to help expand my understanding of that Scripture. I begin and end my study time in prayer.

If we are to grow to be effective, mature Christians in our thoughts and actions, we should never stop studying. Hebrews 5:12 tells us God's Word is alive and active and sharper then a double-edge sword. No matter how many times we've read a Scripture, we can always get something new out of it because it's alive and active.

Just as the Lord told me I had to choose whether or not I believed His Word, we now have to choose whether or not we're going to commit ourselves to studying His Word on a daily basis. I don't want you to have some pushy ophthalmologist question your knowledge and understanding of God's Word and have you come up short like I did.

And by the way, after I'd had that experience with that sweet cardiologist, I told my primary care doctor about what happened. She was the one I'd gone to with the original problem, and she'd referred me to the cardiologist. As I told her what he'd said to me that day, she froze in her tracks and looked stunned.

She said, "I've referred my patients to the same cardiologist for years, and he's a middle-eastern man who is not tall, is not African-American, and who is definitely NOT a Christian. I don't know who you met with that day, but it wasn't the cardiologist I'd referred you to!"

Hmmm, I wonder who it was. Another angel? Jesus? Makes me smile.

Question: Have you turned to medicine, alcohol, food, friends, busyness, pornography, social media, or any other person or vice to numb yourself or medicate your pain?

There's mercy for you if you have! It's not too late. You can turn to God now. Spend time with Him every day, and you'll be amazed at how your life will be transformed. Be patient. It's a process. If you've got "bigger" issues, you might need time with God AND a godly counselor, too.

Endnotes:

1 Psalm 46, NIV.

2 2 Timothy 1:7, NKJV.

3 Jeremiah 29:13, NIV.

4 John 8:32, NKJV.

5 John 16:13, NIV.

6 Dylan, Bob. "Gotta Serve Somebody. Recorded 1979. Columbia Records.

7 I always start my study time by asking the Holy Spirit to speak to me through the Word. I ask Him to direct my thoughts and to teach me what HE wants me to learn that morning. I also say out loud I am submitting my mind to the Lordship and authority of Jesus Christ. I mostly study out of the Amplified Version (AMP), but I also have an English Standard Version (ESV), New International Version (NIV), and New American Standard Version (NASV), which I use for cross-referencing.

CHAPTER 13

Visions Of Babies Danced In His Head

*The moment someone chooses to trust in Jesus Christ, his sins
are wiped away, and he is adopted into God's family. That
individual is set apart as a child of God, with a sacred purpose.* [1]

Jackson

One fall morning Jackson and I were flying down the freeway
in our 1990 silver Toyota Corolla with "Free Fallin'" by Tom Pet-
ty blasting through our speakers. I was enjoying the wind and
loud music, two of my favorite things, when I saw two more of
my favorite things in my rear-view mirror. Jackson's hands were
straight up in the "surrender" position. I looked a little closer and
saw he was singing with his eyes shut and hands raised. I looked
at this beautiful sight the way that only a parent can, with total
unadulterated adoration. I loved him so much, and seeing him
enjoying himself made me feel drunk with joy.

I love this quote I heard once from a speaker:

"God is most glorified when we are most satisfied in Him."

I understood this quote better after becoming a parent. Does anything make a parent happier than to see bliss on her child's face?

When the song ended, I lowered the volume, looked at Jackson in the rear-view mirror and said, "You like that song, huh?

With such a pure spirit Jackson smiled at me and said, "Yeah, I was just worshipping God. I love worshipping God." My heart melted and felt a bit troubled at the same time. I was playing a hedonistic rock ballad and Jackson was using it to worship God. That's who Jackson is. From day one, just as God said, he's been set apart.

He had a total fascination with anything relating to God. He was very obedient and kind. He was an easy child to parent. That was good because after his birth and my near-death experience, I was encountering post-traumatic stress. It was so bad. I had panic attacks daily. I was fearful of EVERYTHING, most of all death because I couldn't imagine leaving this precious boy motherless. If you're a parent, you understand that feeling. I'd never in my life loved anyone or anything like I loved Jackson. His sweet life gave mine a purpose. Although I couldn't see a reason to live for myself, I wanted to live for him. More than living, I wanted to be well for him.

I see Jackson's personality, giftedness, and calmness as a sign of God's grace in my life. I was such an anxious wreck during Jackson's younger years, and I needed him to be easy. Most days I was barely surviving, and Jackson was a sweet, bright spot in an otherwise very onerous time.

When Jackson was just two-years old, he began saying, "God told me..." and then he'd tell us something he felt like God had said to him. I was always blown away by the things he'd known without having any possible way of knowing, other than God's telling him. At the church we attended, they didn't believe God was still speaking. I'd never heard someone say, "God said to me..." at my church. So, the fact that I knew God was talking to me was a little perplexing. Now, Jackson also had an awareness God was speaking to him.

I remember one day Jackson was sitting on his bed right before his nap and he said, "God said that the people are going to die in the fire, so we need to pray that someone helps them." I had no clue what he was talking about. I asked, "What fire?" He didn't know. He just knew there was a fire and people were going to die. So he and I sat on the edge of his little toddler bed and prayed for the people in the fire. Later that night I found out a house had burned to the ground a block away from our house. The family that lived there had almost died, but were rescued at the last minute. I knew why.

Another time, God used him to tell me we needed to leave the church we were attending. Marshall and I had grown up in this denomination, but they didn't believe things like the supernatural gifts still exist, they believe women should be silent and should not have leadership roles, they believe that God is no longer speaking to us, and musical instruments should not be used in worship. Because of these beliefs, Marshall felt we should leave the church.

His reason for wanting to leave was he believed that I had a prophetic gift and was a leader/speaker and would never be fully accepted, nor would my gifts be utilized there. His desire to leave came from his being a loving and esteeming husband.

As sweet as that is, I struggled with not wanting to leave because I had so many relationships there that were important to me. People at that church were like my family, and I couldn't bear the thought of leaving them. Marshall was very patient with me as I resisted the idea for several months. That "family" I didn't want to leave were the very people that ravenously betrayed me when I told on the pastor who'd abused me there.

Then one day out of the blue, Jackson (who had no idea Marshall and I were contemplating leaving our home church) said to me, "Mom, when we go to our new church, you're going to make a lot of friends there. You're going to love our new church."

I was taken back by what he'd said, and I knew he had no idea going to a new church was even a possibility. I asked him to repeat what he'd said and he did, word for word. I asked him what made him say that, and he said, "God told me."

Jackson saying that to me gave me the faith to leave and go to a church where I could thrive and be accepted for who God created me to be.

(About 11 years after we left, we ended up going back to it. After we'd been back for a couple of years, I finally told on my main abuser who was in the role of children's pastor.)

One of my favorite things that happened with Jackson was when I pregnant with our second son. I was so tired, and I wanted every ounce of rest I could get. So one night I got a bowl full of Cheerios and a sippy cup full of water and put it in the hallway floor. It was in the floor where I could see it from my bed and where Jackson would run into it when he came out of his bedroom. My hope was if he saw that, he'd sit down and eat those Cheerios and drink that water, giving me a few more minutes to lie there and wake up slowly. If you've been pregnant, you understand how physically exhausting it can be!

So the next morning, I woke up to Jackson's bedroom door opening. I opened my eyes and saw his sweet little body in his footy pajamas, walk up to the bowl of Cheerios, blanket in tow. I watched, hoping my plan would work. Jackson just stared down at the Cheerios for about 30 seconds, then his mouth fell open like he was surprised by something or he'd suddenly realized something. He then looked straight up at the ceiling, raised his hands and said, "God, thank you for this miracle. Thank you for putting these Cheerios here just for me like You did for the people in Moses' story. I am so glad to have these Cheerios from You. Thank you so much!" He sat down and started eating them and continued talking to God.

It was so precious! Jackson's first thought was, look what God has done for me. He thought these things had been put there supernaturally by God, just for him the way the Israelites were given manna. I loved that. I loved his heart for God. It made my heart swell.

So, God clearly set Jackson apart from the beginning. I think that's why his birth was so difficult. I think that there was a battle over him even entering the world. God has had His hand on Jackson's life. He has such a good heart, a pastor's heart. I love who he is. He's a gift.

Visions of Babies Danced in His Head

When Jackson was six-years old, Marshall and I received a little chunk of money. It wasn't a lot, but we were deciding what we should do with it. We had a thousand different ways it could be spent, so we decided to take a day and fast and pray about it. We wanted God to show us what HE wanted us to do with the money.

We fasted and prayed all day, but neither of us felt like we got any direction. We went to bed a bit discouraged. The next morning we awoke to Jackson standing at our bedside. He said, "God came to me in the night." Up to that point he'd said God had told him things, but he'd never said, "God came to me." We sat up and were intrigued by what he meant. So we asked, "What do you mean?"

"Well, I heard someone saying, 'Jackson, Jackson,' and I thought that it was you guys calling me. But then I realized it was God. You know like in the story about Samuel and Eli?"

Immediately I thought about how God had spoken to me about being pregnant with Jackson using that very story. So I was fascinated Jackson would now be using it in comparison to his own experience.

Jackson continued, "So, I said to God, 'OH, it's YOU!' Then, God showed me a movie while I was in my bed. He showed me a movie of myself taking a bath. Then, I saw these big hands put a little baby into the bath with me. I looked at the baby. It was a brand-new baby, and it was a boy. I began playing with the baby, and then I heard a voice say, 'Jackson, tell your parents to save their money because they're going to need it to adopt this baby that you see now.' And then I realized that the big hands that had put the baby into the bathtub with me were God's hands and this was His voice. So I said 'Okay, God, I will.' Then, the water overflowed out of the bathtub, and it flowed down the hallway, and that's it. That was the end of the movie. So, I came to tell you."

Marshall and I were stunned by this for one main reason -

we had not told Jackson we'd received some money. We had not told Jackson we were praying and fasting and seeking God about what to do with this money. Jackson didn't know. So we knew beyond a shadow of a doubt God had indeed given Jackson this vision as a result of our praying and fasting.

OKAY: But HOW?

So, we set that money aside and began looking into adoption. It's hard when you receive a word from the Lord like that, but you aren't given all the details regarding the "how." So, we decided we'd adopt a little girl since we already had three boys. We also decided we'd adopt a toddler rather than a newborn, since the baby stage was a nightmare to me. As we made our plans and even went through the grueling process of being approved to adopt out of foster care, Jackson would say, "No, that's not what you're supposed to do. You're supposed to adopt a new baby that's a boy. I've seen him. He's a newborn."

It can be tricky receiving a word from God from a six-year old child because you're left to wonder if he heard that exactly right or if he heard something, but then interpreted it through his child-like filter. It can be tough to know if you should take it literally, or just focus on the concept. All my kids hear from the Lord, and sometimes I struggle with how to handle what they hear.

It seemed like every adoption door we knocked on didn't open to us. Two years had gone by from the time Jackson had that vision, and I began feeling extremely discouraged. I started feeling like maybe Jackson had gotten something wrong, or maybe he hadn't heard from God at all. I started thinking maybe we shouldn't adopt another child.

One day I was doing dishes and praying silently in my head, asking God why none of the adoptions we'd tried for worked out. I asked Him if we should stop pursuing adoption. I felt ticked that we'd spent so much time and energy trying to adopt, and I was done. Then, right as I told God all this silently in my mind, Jackson said, "OH, mom! I forgot to tell you something that God told me."

I said, "Oh, yeah, what's that?"

He said, "Remember when God showed me the movie about the baby that we are going to adopt? Remember how the water overflowed and ran down the hallway?" Well, God told me something else about that. About two weeks ago, God told me why the water overflowed and ran down the hallway. He said that the water flowing down the hallway represented time passing. He said that some time would pass from the time He showed me that movie to the time that it happens, but don't lose heart. It IS going to happen!"

I burst into tears! "Jackson, I was JUST praying about that and wondering why it was taking so long! I was starting to think it wasn't going to happen!"

In such a sweet way Jackson said, "Oh no! I'm so sorry I forgot to tell you what God had said to me! If I'd told you then you wouldn't have been worried! I'm so, so sorry!"

About two months later, we adopted our youngest son, Ezekiel Benjamin Hamm. I was there when he was born and was the first one to hold him. God brought him to us through some people at our church. They'd adopted, too and came into our Sunday school class one Sunday to say their birth mom had a friend who was looking to give her baby up for adoption, but hadn't been able to find the right family to take him. As they made this announcement, Jackson walked into our classroom, leaned down and whispered, "I think that's our baby!" I'd already been thinking the same thing. Then, our Sunday school teacher looked at us and mouthed, "I think that's your baby." It was.

The adoption coordinator that orchestrated Ezekiel's adoption told us his birth mom had been *very* picky. She had interviewed countless other couples. Ezekiel's brave birth mom felt like she was supposed to give him to us. She said God told her to. Jackson was right. It was a newborn baby boy we were supposed to adopt.

We later found out Ezekiel's birth mom can see, literally see, into the spirit world. She sees angels and demons and dark and light coming from people. That's her normal. She said when we showed up to meet her, we were full of God's light radiating from us, and we walked into the room with a whole host of angels escorting us in. Because of that she immediately knew we were the ones. The adoption coordinator thought she was unusually picky, but years later we found out she was just looking for the ones that had God's presence and light, literally.

Question: Doesn't that make you wonder what is going on in the spirit world around you right now? Ask God to make you more aware of the spiritual atmosphere around you wherever you go.

Endnote:

1 Charles Stanley, Accessed April 22, 2017, https://www.brainyquote.com/quotes/quotes/c/charlessta451692.html?src=t_family.

CHAPTER 14

Don't Have Your Feelings Hurt, Silly Girl

If love is patient and if love is kind
Oh God give me sign [1]

You might find it easier to believe God cares only about the "big" things, but struggle to believe He cares about the "little" things. I think a lot of people believe that way. He does care about big things, but in my life I've seen proof of Him being very interested in the small things, too. I've come to believe He cares about everything, big, little, and even tiny.

One Christmas our family agreed to not give each other gifts. Everyone was struggling financially, so we gave each other the gift of not giving gifts. That was fine, except I didn't like the idea because I love gifts! I'm all about gifts! Gifts are my "love language." So, I agreed to this no gift giving plan, but I was internally rebelling against it.

176

I did get a gift for my husband, because I hated the idea of his not having anything to open Christmas morning. I thought he'd probably get me a little something, too. But he didn't. Neither did my parents. Neither did any of my boys. Neither did my brother and sister-in-law. There was not even a homemade Christmas card from one of the kids. There was NOTHING for me on Christmas morning, which we'd agreed to. Apparently, I shouldn't have agreed to a gift-less plan when gifts are my love language.

So, after all the kids opened their gifts, I found myself feeling sad. At first I tried to deny that I was sad, but I was. Once I was honest with myself about what I was feeling, I then became mad at myself for feeling sad. I didn't want to be sad, but I was, and I reached a place of accepting that.

The next day I was having quiet time with the Lord, and I told Him how I felt. I said, "Lord, I feel dumb for feeling this way, but the fact that no one did one single little thing for me for Christmas makes me feel unloved and uncared for. I'm just feeling sad, and I need you to help me get over it and feel better."

I poured my heart out to Him and felt a little better just telling Him how I felt. I encourage you to take your pain to God. That's where it can be tended to and healed. Telling Him is always safe, unlike telling people.

So, I wrapped up my time with Him and went upstairs to get ready for the day. When I slipped on my jeans, I found a $20 bill in my pocket! That put a little pep in my step. I set it by my jewelry box and didn't think about it again...until the next morning. I was getting ready and I put on an old jacket I hadn't worn in awhile. Guess what? I found a $20 bill in it. What are the chances of *THAT*? I set it next to the other $20 bill and moved on with my day.

The next day the pants I put on had...you already know, don't you? It had a $20 bill in the pocket. That time I did not just go on with my day. I stopped, a little shocked, and looked up to heaven. I felt God mischievously grinning back at me. That continued for two more days until I had a total of $100. By the fifth day I was overwhelmed by the creative love God expressed to me.

When I found the fifth one, I went into my closet, closed the door and sobbed. "God, what is this? What's going on? Why have I found all this money?"

He spoke so sweetly to me and said, "I wanted to give you a Christmas gift in a unique way because I know how you like excitement and mystery. Now, you've gathered up my Christmas surprise of $100, and I want you to go buy whatever you want with it-on Me. I love you so much. Don't ever doubt you are loved!"

On Christmas my feelings were hurt over something that I'D AGREED TO! I knew they shouldn't have been hurt. The fact I was in a situation I'd put myself in didn't matter to God. He doesn't give us what we deserve. He gives us so much better than we deserve! Notice though, *I took my hurt feelings to God,* admitted my pathetic feelings *and asked Him to tend to me.* One might have thought that He'd just help me with my hurt feelings, but He had a sweeter plan. Remember not just to hope that God will help you, actually ask Him to. Perhaps the fact that I always ask Him for what I need is why I've received some of these miraculous gifts from Him. I ask.

After I just sat in the sweet presence of His love for awhile, I went to Marshall and told him what God told me. Marshall said, "That's amazing. Why don't I be your driver for the day? I'll drive you wherever you want to shop." And he did.

I went to Nordstrom Rack and bought an adorable, brown leather jacket I still wear to this day. It was marked 75% off because of their huge year-end sale. God's timing is always perfect. If He'd given me that money before Christmas, I couldn't have bought that jacket. But because He waited, I got a much nicer gift! God's perfect timing. His timing is not our timing, which is good since ours is imperfect. In order to get the better gift, my gratification had to be delayed a bit.

Giving me money in crazy, mysterious ways to keep my life interesting and exciting because He knows I crave excitement...*That's God!*

For the record, there have been many times when I have taken my pain or hurt feelings to God, and He helps me get over things, but doesn't give me tangible things like He did that Christmas. He'll just tend to my hurting heart. That's more common. That's great too, but this Christmas was extra special.

Sometimes you may find God when you're getting dressed. Sometimes you may find God at a Nordstrom Rack sale. Sometimes you may find God in the place where you lack or have pain or disappointment. I *always* find God in the place where I have lack or pain or disappointment. Are you open to God's doing something unusual in order to show you how much He loves you? He loves you so much. He loves me so much. I have a honey-colored leather jacket to prove it.

Me in the leather jacket that God gave me for Christmas.

Question: Do you have any hurt feelings you need to ask God to tend to? Even if you think it's silly, ask Him to apply His therapeutic treatment to your hurting heart. Ask, and keep on asking. (Luke 18:1 AMP)

Endnote:

1 Brian Howes, Luke Smallbone, Joel Smallbone, Tedd Tjorhom. "This Is Love." Recorded 2016. Fervent/Curb.

CHAPTER 15

Diving Into The Deep

Wish you could go back and tell yourself what you know now [1]

Seventeen years and four months after that miraculously eventful day when I prayed with Father John and was taken to heaven, I was walking down the hallway of a home my family had just moved into. This was four months after the prophetic Texan had told me, "After this trip, everything is going to change for you, *everything*. One year from now your life will be unrecognizable to you."

Remember, tenth move in 17 years? As I walked down the hall of this new house, I had a random thought (or so it seemed): "If I needed to deal with the darkness that was loitering in the corner of my 'heavenly light' dream, I could handle that now. I could now face my demons, *if I had to*." What that meant to me was this: "IF God says I HAVE to tell someone about the abuse

I've been through, I could handle it now." This was the first time I'd ever even entertained the thought of telling anyone what I'd been through.

Then I continued down the hall, thinking absolutely nothing of it. After all, I was pretty sure I did *not* need to "deal with it" because I was fine, just fine, perfectly *fine*.

A couple of days later, my son and I were at a Christian ministry and counseling center. This place was known for godly counsel, demonic deliverance, and a prayer ministry that seemed to have some real authority with results. They actually believed what the Bible said about these subjects.

Unfortunately, finding a place like this is no small task. Few Christian churches or ministries operate with the high-level spiritual authority that God intended for *all* Christians to operate with. (See John 14:12 and Mark 6:7, and12, Luke 10:19.) This place did. I'd gone to some of their prayer gatherings and had found them to be the real deal. They were broaching subjects most churches wouldn't touch with a ten-foot pole. They addressed things like satanic preschools and what we should do about it.

One hot June afternoon I was in a session with one of our sons. The counselor asked him to step out of the room, so we could talk privately. At first, we spoke about him and the issues at hand. But then, I shared a story with her I felt was somehow connected to his issues. That story led to another. Before I knew it, we'd visited for almost an hour! I'd shared a handful of my life's events from my treasure trove, but didn't think much of it. They were my life, my "normal," my one and only reality...*or so I thought.*

Towards the end of story-telling hour, the counselor looked at me in a way that made me uneasy. She said, "I'm trying to think of how to say this. I don't want to understate it, and I don't want to overstate it." Now I was completely on edge.

"Okay," I said, unsure of what she could possibly be getting ready to say. I braced myself. "The things that you just shared with me...they're...*not normal*. I'm sure that you know that though."

I certainly *didn't* know that! Wasn't I just sharing some of my "God stories" the way that *any* believer could share? My eyes looked to the corner of the room as my soul attempted to make room for what she was saying.

She continued to affirm me, but said there seemed to be something that was holding me back, perhaps something painful from my past I'd not dealt with.

Because I had just been walking down my hallway at home thinking "I could deal with *that* darkness, *if I needed to*," I was quite taken back by this! She obviously had no idea I had *just* thought that. She didn't know my family of origin or anything about my past.

She said she'd be happy to see me if I ever wanted to talk through anything. That very moment I remembered a dream I'd had about six months earlier, several months before I'd even met this woman.

In my dream I was at some sort of conference. There was a podium where someone was going to be speaking, but no one was going up to it. I started to think I should do something, take charge. I got up and looked around the room to see if I could get things going. Then I saw this woman (this counselor now sitting before me). At the time of this dream, I had seen her and knew of her, but had never met her. So, in the dream I saw her and thought, "If *she's* here, then I don't need to worry. She has more authority than I do, so I can rest knowing that she's here." I had a strong sense I could trust her and she was safe. So, feeling relieved she was there, I sat back down.

Then, I saw people walking into the room carrying large canvases with beautiful colors of green, red, and blue painted on them. I stretched my neck and saw painted on them the words "BE COURAGE." Be courage? That doesn't make sense. It should say "Be courageous" or "Have courage," but not *"Be courage."* I thought that it was odd, but knew I *really* wanted one.

Then I understood the only way to get one was to earn it by "being courage," more specifically one had to be courage on display.

I noticed there was still no speaker at the podium, so I looked over at this counselor, pointed to the podium and mouthed, "Are you going to speak?" She pointed to me and mouthed back, "No, *you* are." I knew the way I could get one of the "BE COURAGE" signs would be by speaking. Determined I could trust this woman's direction to me, I stood up to go to the podium. Then, I woke up.

So, I remember the dream as I sat in her office and heard her offer to "listen if I ever want to talk." I also connected her offer to the fact I'd just thought I could handle dealing with hard things from my past if I needed to, if God made me, and this was probably not a coincidence. It had God's name written all over it. He certainly had my attention, and I began to feel very curious about what He was doing here. I thanked her for her offer and headed home with my son.

184

That Girl Looks Sad

Two days later, my 11-year-old son called me into the room and excitedly pointed to the TV screen. "Look! Look what I found! Your old home movies from when you were a little girl! Look at yourself!"

Feeling his excitement as my own, I turned to the TV to watch the girl in the video. She was at summer camp, and the first thing I noticed was the extreme sadness in her eyes...sadness as if she wished she were dead. Deep, gut-wrenching, crushing, suffocating sadness.

The next thing I noticed was her perm. She was rocking those artificial curls like nobody's business. Her hair hadn't been died yet, so it was dark brown. She was cute and looked like the girl version of my son who was showing me the video. Somehow comparing her to my son made my heart lament, but I didn't know why. I began to ache for her, and my belly started filling with internal tears as it had so many times before. It was as if there was a mini-me inside that was crying. I felt so very heart-sick for her...her, *not me, her.* It truly felt like that was someone else I was looking at. Although, part of my brain understood it was indeed me, it didn't *feel* like me, and I didn't understand why.

Tears brimmed my eyes, and I left the room, quickly making my way to my bedroom closet and began to sob softly. Why am I crying? What on earth am I feeling? I sobbed into my husband's T-shirt to muffle my cries. I felt so strange and knew it was just a matter of time before my husband came in and asked what happened, why I left the room crying. I would have no answer because I didn't know. Seeing that girl in the old home video triggered a deep sense of anguish, but I couldn't fully wrap my brain around *why.*

I had to pull it together because we were getting ready to go to my nephew's 3-year-old birthday party. I washed my face and put my sunglasses on (which worked well because it was a pool party). In the car someone put on "Fifteen" by Taylor Swift. More tears. I looked out the window, wiping the saltwater drops steadily rolling down my cheeks. They're rolling again now as I write.

"Mom, are you okay?" Ethan asked with obvious concern and an adorable, awkward smile that he has when he's feeling uncomfortable or nervous.

I cleared my throat to try to choke out a voice that didn't sound as disturbed as it actually was. "Yes."

"Why are you crying then? What's wrong?" Ethan continued probing.

I quickly prayed for an answer that was appropriate for my 8, 11, 13, and 16- year old sons to hear. My husband looked at me with concern and curiosity, too.

"It's just that seeing that home video…" I broke into a soft sob. I could see fear in my sons' eyes and tried to reconfigure what I was feeling into something they could handle.

"It's just that seeing that home video made me feel sad. I was just thinking about some of the hard things that the girl in the video was dealing with in her life, and some of the hard things that were still ahead of her. I was wishing that I could give her a hug to comfort her. I'd like to give her a heads-up about what was still to come for her. But, really, I'm okay. Just thinking about some kind of sad stuff, that's all."

I forced a smile, hoping it would hide the tornado that was swirling through my soul.

"Oh, okay. Are you *sure* you're okay? I'm sorry your home movie made you sad. I thought it would make you happy. Is this song making you sad, too? We can change it!" Ethan offered.

"It's okay. Thank you, precious." I turned my face so he could no longer see my expression, because I could no longer control it. My face muscles involuntarily contorted and forced my face to show the truth of the matter: I was painfully aware that scared little girl in the video had already experienced hell on earth, yet, the worst was still to come for her. I *felt* her heinous reality in a way I never had before. In that moment her feelings were upon me like a tidal wave.

We continued to drive. I turned the music up so no one could hear my cries. Life was imitating art, or the other way around as Taylor sang,

When you're 15 and somebody tells you they love you,
you're going to believe them. [1]

I continued thinking of the girl in the video. At 15 she'd been told she was loved by that pastor with the cat poop hair and the ugly mustache. Why didn't the other adults in her life see how sad she was? I had an overwhelming desire to hug her and stroke her hair and tell her there would be some more dark years ahead, but ultimately everything was going to be okay. *She* was going to be okay. She was going to survive the valley of the shadow of death, both figuratively and literally.

But, unfortunately, I couldn't hug her. As sad as she was, she would have to exist in her pain, all alone, uncomforted and unacknowledged. There wasn't going to be an adult in her life that would see past her facade to her truth. I then began to feel angry at how blind her parents had been. They were so wrapped up in their own issues they were oblivious to hers. How lonely and unprotected she was. As bad off as she was, it'd be another couple years before the darkest years would begin, and that darkness would come through the hands of that pastor who was at that summer camp with her.

As we drove to my nephew's birthday party, all I wanted to do was go back and yell at that girl on the TV screen, "RUN! RUN AS FAST AS YOU CAN! Hurry, leave! You're not safe!"

The desire to go back in time and comfort her was overwhelming. Although, in a weird way, I perceived I was comforting her in that moment. In some unexplainable way, I was comforting her just by acknowledging her pain...for the first time....ever.

The Checklist

Two days passed from seeing that video. My husband was at work and my kids were all home for the first day of what would turn out to be a life-altering summer vacation. I sat in my comfy bed with fluffy pillows on every side supporting my mushy, aging body. I sipped my coffee as I watched "The Joni Lamb Show," as I did most mornings. They were interviewing a pastor from one of my favorite churches, Gateway Church in Dallas, Texas. At first they were making small talk and being humorous, and I laughed along. Then, in an instant, the mood shifted and he began talking about how he was molested when he was a child. He went through a checklist of things he'd always told himself regarding the abuse, things like:

1.   Unfortunate things happen to all of us.

2.   It's over now.

3.   I just need to forgive, forget, and move on. That's what

good Christians do.

4. There's nothing that anyone can do about it now, so no need to tell anyone.

5. I'm doing fine now, so I should just try to forget about it.

I was stunned. That was the *same* checklist of things I'd always told myself. Tears AGAIN! At that point in my life I was not an emotional person at all, so all these tears were strange to me! I sat my cup of coffee down and wailed, as I continued to listen to this pastor tell his truth, and it was remarkably similar to mine. I could not stop the flood of tears. It felt like a dam broke in my spirit. Thank God, my boys all stayed out of my room as I cried and cried *and cried*.

My tears turned into prayer. I looked up and said, "What are You asking of me here? Do I *need* to tell someone about this? Do I *have to* tell? Why are You forcing me to think about this? *WHY?*"

God knew what I was really asking. I was asking Him if I could be whole and healthy without telling anyone about the molestation and abuse I'd endured. Very clearly He impressed upon my spirit to tell Marshall (my husband) and then my parents. I first told Marshall, and he responded with complete love and compassion, as I'd expected. My husband, being a wounded one too, had a vast capacity to understand pain. He was so loving and tender to me.

Then, I texted my parents who, as you might have guessed, are deeply wounded ones as well. I asked if they could come over because I needed to tell them something. I knew I would lose my courage if I didn't text them immediately. They responded immediately they would come that afternoon at 2:00. Seeing their response made me feel like I was going to throw up. Telling them would be worse than telling Marshall.

Having so much pain and never speaking of it was a heavy load to carry. I had so many secrets I'd never felt my parents could handle. When I'd done little "test runs" in the past, they showed me they could not handle it. So I continued to carry the load alone, so alone. I always felt completely alone. In a room crowded with people, I felt the sting of forsaken isolation. I felt like no one could relate to me, like I was so weird. I think most of us who have been through traumatic things feel this way.

Even if you tell someone of the pain, they can't jump into it with you. So feeling alone *is* a reality in a way, not just a perception. It's like you live in a glass room that has curtains all around it. You can pull the curtains back for someone to see in, but they can't actually enter the room with you. They can just peer in, and maybe attempt to understand you better on some microscopic level. Later I would find that when I shared my truth with a friend whose truth was similar to mine was the least alone I would ever feel.

Maybe you know what I'm talking about? Have you ever gone through something so painful that as much as people tried to understand, they really couldn't and you felt so alone? I think that pain has a way of making us feel isolated, especially if the pain is accompanied by shame. That's a trying thing for wounded ones to endure, the loneliness of it. Only God really knows, understands, and can be in the pain with us. If you've been disappointed that a human couldn't go there with you, perhaps today is the day to let him off the hook. No human can fully be in a tragedy with you. Only God can....and He always is.

So, the clock was ticking. My parents' lives were more stable than they had ever been, and I felt maybe now they could *final-*

ly handle the darkness that would be presented to them. I was filled with both dread and an odd sense of hope. I was 37 years and 9 months old, and today at 2:00 pm I was going to tell.

Question: Is there anything that has happened in your life you've kept a secret? Have you ever told yourself: "I'm fine now. I don't need to tell anyone about *that*. It's over. Just move on. Others couldn't handle it if I told them about *that*."

Ask God to show you if you have anything HE wants you to tell someone. Remember, the secrets we maintain are usually Satan's playground.

Endnote:

1 Swift, Taylor. "Fifteen." Recorded 2008. Big Machine.

CHAPTER 16

A Time To Tell

A Time for Everything
For everything there is a season, and a time for every matter
under heaven:
a time to be born, and a time to die;
a time to plant, and a time to pluck up what is planted;
a time to kill, and a time to heal;
a time to break down, and a time to build up;
a time to weep, and a time to laugh;
a time to mourn, and a time to dance;
a time to cast away stones, and a time to gather stones together;
a time to embrace, and a time to refrain from embracing;
a time to seek, and a time to lose;
a time to keep, and a time to cast away;
a time to tear, and a time to sew;
a time to keep silence, and a time to speak;
a time to love, and a time to hate;
a time for war, and a time for peace. [1]

And for me there came a time to tell...

The doorbell rang at 2:00 sharp! One of my boys answered the door and I heard my mom's voice. I prayed for strength as my stomach turned. I took a cleansing breath as if I was about to give birth.

I went out to meet them and instructed the boys to give us some time without interruption. Then I led them to my bedroom. Tense and nauseous, I called on "Courageous Girl."

My dad sat in the brown, leather Lazy Boy, the same one I sit in now as I write. My mom grabbed my blue desk chair and pulled it around to be by my dad. I sat on my bed comforter hoping it would live up to its name, as I needed comfort. It's all shades of blue-just like I felt. Grabbing a down pillow to put over my lap for comfort or protection or something, I took another cleansing breath, and *PUSH*....

"I have something difficult to tell you. I never planned on telling you, but God very clearly told me to tell you now. So I am. There are some things that have happened to me that are dark, sad, bad. I'd always felt these things are so horrible and they would make anyone who heard them feel sad. I reasoned that we didn't need to *all* feel sad, so I would just take one for the team. I also had a sense that you wouldn't be able to handle this information as your lives were so chaotic and unstable. But now, maybe you can handle it?"

My mom had a troubled look on her face. My dad looked cool as a cucumber. I paused the introduction to my Nightmare 101 course, and my mom said, *"Okay?"*

"Okay," I continued. I began to tell them about my initiation into the world of those who have been abused, or at least as much as I was conscious of at that point. In counseling I began remembering a lot more. I told them about incidents that happen to me starting at a very young age. At that point I had three main, unfortunate things to tell them about. Actually, "unfortunate" is really not an appropriate word. Horrific is more adequate.

But then came the worst news; the information about our close family friend that was also a pastor at our church. I'll change his name to protect his children and wife who don't deserve the shame he brought on them. Even though his wife and kids have spoken horribly about me, I know they're speaking from ignorance, and someday they'll know that.

"There are things about 'Chuck' I've never told you about." The expressions on their faces changed. I could see they were gearing up for what they were going to hear. I went on to tell them that our supposed close family friend had been my worst, on-going abuser. I told them about the beginning stages of the abuse when he started grooming me, then of the subsequent stages where he had an ongoing sexual relationship with me. I explained about the most recent of stages where, even though we were both married, he'd try to mess with my mind and say inappropriate things.

I told my parents that this pastor was a sick, potentially evil man, and I was no longer going to be the keeper of his secrets. My parents agreed with my assessment of him being sick and potentially evil.

Thankfully, my parents did not dismiss me at all. They immediately knew in their gut that the tragic information was true. They admitted they made poor decisions and did not protect me enough. My dad profusely apologized to me, and took his part of the blame. My mom questioned her judgement regarding an out-of-state trip they'd let me take with him all alone when I was 14.

Not all of us who tell on our abusers are as fortunate in these revealing conversations. I was so grateful my parents believed me. Often people who tell about their abuse aren't believed by those closest to them. If you weren't believed when you told on your abuser, I'm so sorry! That's sad the people you told were so ignorant. What they don't know is people *rarely* make this kind of stuff up. They don't realize how it took every ounce of your strength and courage to finally tell. On behalf of knowledgeable, compassionate, human beings who have a clue, I am so sorry you had the guts to tell, but weren't believed. I'm so, so sorry! If you weren't believed, there are many extra gifts waiting for you. Ask God to give them to you. Ask God for justice. Ask God for redemption.

My dad suggested I go to counseling to talk about what I had just revealed, even though I kept claiming, "I'm okay, really!" He said that he'd pay for my first two sessions and handed me the $220 cash on the spot.

Rotten Fruit

I accepted the money from my dad and agreed to talk to a counselor, even though I really didn't think that I needed to. I had already gone to a lot of counseling to deal with the *fruit* of sexual abuse. Some of the "fruit" grown on the abuse trees are depression, anxiety, shame, nightmares, social phobias, eating disorders, suicidal tendencies, irrational fears, cutting, and self-hatred. I'd gone to counseling attempting to get free from my toxic fruit which consisted of several, but not all, of these things.

I never even hinted at the truth of my abuse history to any counselor I'd seen before I told my husband and parents about it. This is crazy, but I remember feeling too ashamed to. I know, that's what they do! Counselors help you with that shame, but I couldn't bring myself to utter the words. So I'd go to counselors and have them help me with fear, but never talk about where the fear came from. Honestly, I never really thought all that toxic fruit was connected to the molestation and abuse. I thought it hadn't affected me. That seems so bizarre now, but somehow that's what I believed. Have you ever downplayed or rationalized something to make it more palatable? That's what I was doing.

Counseling had actually been somewhat helpful to me even without acknowledging the abuse. Along with going to counseling, I'd also run hard and fast into God's arms and talked to Him about things. He'd healed a lot of hurt in me already, so I really didn't feel I needed to drag up the gory details and talk about them with this counselor. My dad suggested I might be wrong, so I agreed to go. Plus, he was paying for two sessions. I figured two sessions would be plenty.

The Morning After

Immediately following our conversation, I felt like telling them was the right thing to do. The next morning was a different story completely! I'd wished I could take it all back. I felt so exposed and vulnerable and angry that I'd said anything. My silence had been my protection – protection from judgment, speculation, prying, probing, labeling, pity, and more shame than I already had. I had always maintained a belief if no one knew how defiled I was and perceived me as pure, then I could continue to feel pure. "The morning after" that long held belief appeared to be true. Now that my husband and parents knew, I felt impure, shameful, and vulnerable. I *loathed* these feelings. They didn't have a "morning after" pill for this kind of thing!

It's hard to describe the feelings of that day. In some ways the abuse that I'd endured felt real for the first time in my life. My mind had involuntarily created complex, mental infrastructures to make it *feel* like it had happened to someone else. It was as if reality didn't matter as long as it didn't *feel* real. By not telling anyone, I could deceive myself, keep myself numb, and keep it from feeling real. Again, I was not consciously doing any of that. The things that had happened to me and my thoughts about it had usually stayed at a subconscious level.

There were some holes in my theory of "Not telling solves your problems." Throughout the years, not telling had caused me several problems. One was that suddenly out of the thick, black numbness I'd hear the break out sounds of internal sobs. I would hear the sound of someone crying all the time in my head. I would learn that those crying sounds were coming from the broken parts inside of me that were scared, and so, so, SO sad.

The crying came from the parts of me that had been created to deal with sexual trauma. *Some* of the sadness lifted the day that I told, and "they" felt honored, honored to be acknowledged. "They" being the parts of me that had dealt with the worst of the sexual abuse. They'd waited for this day for a very, very long time. They'd been through so much, and it was finally their day to be recognized for all they did to keep me going and protect me from feeling the worst of it.

Keith Urban's music ministered to me that first day after telling. God can use anything or anyone to minister to one of His hurting children. I spent the entire day after "I told" lying in my closet with the lights out and a towel across the bottom of the door to block the light so I couldn't see my own hand in front of my face. Any light at all seemed too offensive to my weary, watering, pain-filled eyes.

As I laid on my closet floor, I listened to every Keith Urban song I had on my i-pod twice (59 songs in all, *twice*). I sensed maybe Keith and his beautiful wife were wounded ones who'd also had a lot of hurts. I thought the same thing about John Mayer and Jackson Browne. Their lyrics take the groans of my suffering heart and set them to a tempo that makes it all palatable. That's the beauty of artistic expression. It expresses what we feel in an inspired way, doesn't it?

Some of John Mayer's lyrics make me think he's been through the *exact same* things I have. I sing along to his music, and my achy, fatigued soul finds relief. I'm quite the escape artist when pain comes on the scene. When I needed to escape, music was my vehicle of choice. I used music often to float out of reality, because sometimes reality ain't all it's cracked up to be. That makes me think of something Reba McEntire once said, "For me, singing sad songs often has a way of healing a situation. It gets the hurt out in the open into the light, out of the darkness." [2]

The day after telling, I also listened to a lot of John Mayer music, and I heard him sing this:

> *Well it sucks to be honest, and it hurts to be real.*
> *But it's nice to make some love that I can finally feel.* [3]

I hoped John was right. I hoped at some point there would be an upside to honesty, an upside to not being numb. At that point I just felt pain, but I hoped someday I might make love that I could actually feel. So, I sang along and for brief moments that gifted me some relief. Relief because I felt understood.... albeit by a stranger, a singer/song writer I'd never met. Until a wounded person goes through the healing process, those closest to him never *really* know him. Pre-healed, wounded warriors are most at home among perfect strangers. I'd literally felt most comfortable when I was in a foreign city, surrounded by aliens.

Question: At the end of the last chapter did God reveal anything to you that you need to tell someone? If so, ask God to prepare the hearts of the people you need to tell. When I told my parents about "Chuck" (the pastor that abused me), they said they had *just* had a conversation about how my dad was sensing something was really wrong with "Chuck. He'd just asked my mom to stay away from him because he could tell Chuck had something very perverse about him. When my dad said that, I knew God had been preparing my parents to believe what I was going to tell them that day. Ask Him to do that for you now.

Endnotes:

1 Ecclesiastes 3:3-8 (ESV).

2 McEntire, Reba. Accessed April 2, 2017. https://www.brainyquote.com/quotes/quotes/r/rebamcenti163526.html

3 Mayer, John. "Shadow Days." Recorded 2012. Columbia Records.

CHAPTER 17

Courage On Display

Healing takes courage, and we all have courage,
even if we have to dig a little to find it. [1]

I took my dad's advice (and his $220) and went to counseling. Naively, I thought I could probably go to two sessions and then I'd be good to go. It took a *lot* more than that! There was so much I had blocked out of my conscious memory, and a lot of it started coming back up as soon as I went to counseling. I had much more to deal with than I'd originally realized.

As I walked out of my first counseling session, I was in a state of shock. I mean I was literally, physically in shock. My head was swirling around like a child spinning in a grassy field. My whole body felt pins and needles that weren't there. I was having a hard time speaking – I literally had nothing to say. Each breath felt laborious. I was in shock the way one is when they've just been in a car accident.

As we got into the car to leave the counseling center, I wanted to recoil from the can of worms I'd just opened. I just wanted to fly away to a safer, gentler place. Because I knew flying to safety wasn't an option, I'd hoped I'd get lucky and be killed in a head-on collision on my way home. I wanted to retract every word I'd just spoken to my counselor and slip back into the cowardice of deception and denial. But there was also that teeny tiny part of me that hoped maybe, just maybe, I was headed towards true freedom for the first time in my life. Even with that glimmer of hope, the predominate emotions I was experiencing were terror and dread.

I tried to wrap my brain around what was happening, but didn't seem capable of that task. Despite my desires to, I didn't get to fly away that day, and I wasn't killed by a head-on either. I didn't retract my words, and I didn't allow myself the luxury of being a coward. I persisted in the work of being vulnerable and finding healing.

My courage was not void of substantial points of weakness. During my counseling process, I medicated my pain with food and alcohol. I gained twelve pounds during this season. I'd love to say I lived on faith alone during these months, but I didn't. I used these vices to cope. Should I lie about how I managed my soul-degrading pain during those black months to forego being judged? No. I'd do a great disservice to you and to myself if I lied about this. I can't be free when I'm lying. Telling the truth is liberating, even if the truth is unpleasant. If I lied to you about this issue, I'd imprison myself again, and I've worked too hard to re-imprison myself now. When we're honest, it gives permission to others to be their true selves as well. My truth is that I used food and alcohol to manage the blackest months of my life.

As I medicated myself I learned that *every* vice has a negative side-effect. It's only when we cope with things God's way that we'll be able to escape unfavorable side-effects. Every other coping mechanism will be harmful to us in some way. I love the way singer-songwriter Justin Timberlake expresses how alcohol won't solve our problems. Take a look at the lyrics in his song, "Drink You Away":

> The bottom of the bottle to fill this empty heart up
> A thousand proof don't change the truth, I dive in, but I can't
> I can't drink you away
> I've tried Jack, I've tried Jim, I've tried all of their friends
> But I can't drink you away
> All of these rocks, I can't swim outta this skin, I'm livin' in [2]

When we wake up in the morning, we discover that our vice didn't take our pain away. In fact, sometimes our pain is worse after we've used a vice. The morning after we're still living in the same skin. Every single vice that we use to numb or escape our pain will leave us more empty than we were before. It does give temporary relief, and thus the lure.

As the counseling process progressed, I kept asking my counselor, "Now why do I want to deal with all of this again? Why is it helpful to process through this pain instead of just 'moving on' and forgetting about it? Why is it worth it? I've felt numb to the pain of my abuse for so long, and I don't necessarily want to remove my emotional Novocain pump unless the payoff will be significant!"

My counselor would then remind me of some truths. One, you don't get to selectively numb yourself. If you choose to numb your pain, you're simultaneously numbing yourself to some good emotions as well. That means you're always living at an emotionally dumbed down, muted level. You could say you're living in sepia instead of in color. The only way to live life to the full, and to experience a healthy range of emotions is to process through the trauma you've been through. Somehow, I knew that she was right, and I really wanted to live life in color, not in sepia.

Two, childhood traumas will always affect us in ways we don't even know we're affected. Childhood trauma inserts beliefs, fears, ways of thinking, and operating deep into our soul before we mature enough to know what's what. That's why so many of us don't even think we've been through anything that needs healing. Our reality is all we've ever known, so we don't know just how wrong it is. Or sometimes we know we have a certain struggle, but we don't realize that struggle is directly connected to something from our childhood. The counseling process helps us to connect the dots.

Working through our traumas will inadvertently untangle and remove the cobwebs in our soul. If we don't deal with our wounds, we will never live the abundant life God intended for us to live. We'll keep having the same problems, going around the same mountains until we deal with the *source* of our pain. We'll keep having the same kind of struggles, the same kind of failures over and over.

Often we'll have the same kind of weirdos attracted to us, or we'll be attracted to the same kind of weirdos because our wounds distort our desires. We'll tend to hit a glass ceiling, and we won't even know why. As I listened to my counselor explain how processing our pain leads to a freer, healthier life, I reached down and disconnected my Novocain pump.

The thought of not *fully living* was so dreadful to me. The reasons she gave for why I should process through my pain resonated. I knew I *had* hit that glass ceiling, and I wasn't living the fullest life possible. There's something about having secrets that holds you hostage. Secrets make you a prisoner, but at some point you'll look down and realize you have the prison keys in your hand.

For some of us, our emotional prison is all we've known. We don't know if we could make it in the real world. So we hold the keys, but never use them. You know the type, the person who is so obviously broken, but isn't getting the help she needs. I can think of several people right now who need counseling in the worst way, but day after day they just stare at their prison cell keys and say, "I'm fine. Really, fine."

It Gets Worse Before It Gets Better
Don't wish it away. Don't look at it like it's forever.
I can honestly say that things can only get better. [3]

I've found in healing, it often gets worse before it gets better. But then it *does* get better, so much better. In my situation, where I was taking the lid off a host of things, I'd utterly forgotten or just not consciously thought about for decades, it had to get worse before it got better. As you let those traumatic memories rise up to the conscious level, you have to *feel some* of the pain you'd tried to avoid, forget, or numb for years. This requires courage and a pain management program. It also requires you to be patient while it gets worse before it gets better.

So, my Novocain pump was out and there was tingling as the numbness faded. Cue the dramatic music as painful memories entered stage right. Every Tuesday I went go to my counselor's office and took a seat in the movie theater of my mind. The theater operator pushed "Play," and I watched memories that looked like the kind of horror films I'd intentionally never watched. Apart from the day these memories were made, I'd had nothing to do with them until this process.

I had memories come to me outside of counseling, as well. Some of them I could process on my own with God, but most were too dark to work through apart from the assistance of a seasoned counselor. When a memory came to me outside of counseling, I would stop and pray, "Lord, is this something we can deal with now, or should I wait until counseling?" He'd always direct me. Sometimes I'd go into my closet and the Lord and I talked through a memory. I've cried a river in that closet!

There were a lot of tears from the sheer pain of the memories. But there were also a lot of tears from grieving the person I'd thought I was. I was coming to terms with a whole new reality about myself. I cried over the innocence that was stolen from me at such a young age. I cried on behalf of the internal "mini-me's" that had never been able to cry because they just had to suck it up and deal with it at the time.

I cried over the things I'd witnessed that no one, especially no child, should ever see. I cried over the years of my life that had been stolen from me. I cried over how I would now be perceived. I cried over the realization that I was so unprotected.

I'm not normally a big crier. I'm not super emotional, but during this season I cried in session. I cried out of session. I cried in my closet. I cried in my car. I cried in my dreams. *I cried.* As I cried, it felt like the toxins of trauma were being flushed out with each tear.

As hard as it was to go through this process, it's important you know this: after every single session I was freer than I was when I walked in! Sometimes I was *a lot* freer! Depending on how much we accomplished in a session, sometimes I'd walk out feeling the weight of the world I'd carried for years was actually, finally gone! I started having a peace I'd never known. I started having a joy I'd really never known! I started to feel, good and bad-I felt it all. I discovered it's worth it to feel. The pain of the healing process is worth the reward of being healed. The highs are worth the lows.

Use Your Words

As my process progressed my counselor encouraged me to tell my church leaders about what the pastor had done to me. He was still on staff, and was now the children's pastor. That meant he had ample opportunity to do this to someone else, if I didn't tell. This decision was HUGE and weighed on me heavily. I didn't have anything to gain by telling. In fact, telling would cause me substantial loss.

When I started the counseling process, I had no intention of telling. I only planned on getting healing for myself. But as the reality of what this man had done to me was unveiled, my counselor urged me to tell the church leaders and the police! I did *NOT* want to!

I contemplated his wife's and children's lives, and how they were innocent. It was horrible to think about how revealing this man's actions would probably be excruciating to his family, and how horrible it would be to hear these things about someone you love. I felt so sorry for his wife and sons, as it was unfair that what he had done was going to bring devastation and grief into their lives. They didn't deserve that! Although, I believe we tend to know the truth in our guts, even when we don't know it with our brains. I believe his wife knew and still knows deep inside she's married to a screwed-up man.

I thought about how telling would most likely cost him his job. This was the only career he'd had. I also considered how I'd be viewed after telling. I tried to count the cost of telling. What I discovered is there's no way to fully count the cost of a situation that has so many variables. Might he be ready to confess himself? Might he walk in the light and acknowledge what he'd done? Or, would he lie and attack me out of an attempt to self-preserve? Would the church leaders sweep it under the rug as they had with other sin-filled situations? Would the leaders believe me? How would the church members respond? Would the other girls he's been immoral with share what happened with them? At that time, four other girls admitted he'd been immoral with them. Now as I'm writing this I've heard from seven girls he's been immoral with, and I know there are more. Would they have the courage to share?

I weighed the cost of telling as best I could, which I found out later, was not very well.

After weighing it all out I ended up deciding I must tell. It became a matter of right and wrong to me. Telling was right. Not telling was wrong. It was that black and white to me. There were three adorable little girls around 10-years old that were under this man's leadership in children's ministries. I was 10-years old the first time he'd been inappropriate with me. I knew if I didn't tell, I was leaving them vulnerable. I couldn't live with that.

Telling my parents and husband was very hard, but telling my church leaders would be monumentally harder. First, my husband and I met with our senior pastor and told him. He responded with love and said he believed me. Then, he arranged a meeting with some of the elder board, himself, my husband, my mom, the wife of one of the elders (for moral support) and me. We met at our pastor's house.

The day of the meeting it was hard for me to breathe. My muscles felt heavy and each step felt difficult. I had pressure in my chest I'd hoped was a brewing heart attack that would take my life *before* the meeting. My shoulders were tense. My scalp was tingly. I had a pounding headache and felt scared and embarrassed. I couldn't eat. I felt dizzy and nauseous. The day was *grueling and felt oh so long!* I just kept telling myself that I was doing this for other little girls that could be his victims if I didn't tell. I was also doing it for "Little Me" who had gone through hell because of this man. She deserved to be heard.

An Agonizing Day

The minutes went by like hours. My husband, mom, dad, and I went to dinner before the meeting. I could barely choke down enough food to keep my blood sugar from plummeting. I'd heard a shot of Tequila referred to as a "shot of courage," and I was tempted to test out that notion. I knew that I needed to be fully sober and of clear, sound mind, so I resisted. I was mustering every ounce of courage I had, but it just didn't feel sufficient. If I ever needed a shot of courage, it was now.

As I tried to distract myself from the irreversible plank I was getting ready to walk, I thought of that dream I'd had a few months earlier. "BE COURAGE!" I would tell myself. I thought about that dream as I sat waiting to go before a room full of men and share something so humiliating and personal. Many of these men I'd known my whole life, and they were twice my age. I needed to *be* courage, the embodiment of it, courage on display.

I also thought about how God knew this day was coming, even though I'd had no clue. He knew, and He warned and prepared me through a series of dreams. I thought about 2 Corinthians 12:9 (NIV), "My grace is sufficient for you, for my power is made perfect in weakness. Therefore I will boast all the more gladly about my weaknesses, so that Christ's power may rest on me." This Scripture was particularly meaningful to me this day because I felt so weak, so scared.

On this long, loathsome day I wondered if I'd ever taste wild honey again. Each minute of the day I was using everything I had to breathe, exist, survive. I couldn't even remember how to find wild honey, let alone what it tasted like.

Dreams

As I looked back on my dreams of the previous months, there were many that had directed my path. The main way God speaks to me is through dreams. God spoke to people using dreams throughout Scripture. I don't understand why people don't pay close attention to their dreams. God will show you a lot through them if you'll pay attention. Dreams tend to be symbolic, and only occasionally literal. In the book *Who Switched Off My Brain?* Dr. Caroline Leaf, Ph.D, says this:

In fact, dreams often feel strange because during the day we process from concrete to abstract, while at night, we process the other way around-from abstract to concrete. There is a kind "thinking" behind dreams, but as abstract ideas, visually represented and confusing. Furthermore, because of the biochemical of emotion, dreams not only have content but feelings as well. 4

This shows us why dreams can seem confusing. If we are taking them literally when actually they are more abstract or symbolic, we will miss the message the Dream-Giver is trying to give. Once we consider that most of the time they are symbolic with metaphorical messages, they become easier to interpret.

God uses symbols so those who have a genuine desire to understand the deep things of God can search out the meanings of the symbols and find the message. Throughout Scripture there is metaphoric language with hidden truths that must be searched out. They are not necessarily in plain sight. Symbolic messaging is a way of screening out the bottom feeders. That's not how God would say it. That's how I'm saying it. It's a way to separate those who really want to know the deep things of God, from those who would only take the information if they didn't have to work for it, if it was cheap. Take a look at Proverbs 25:2 (NIV):

> It is the glory of God to conceal a matter;
> to search out a matter is the glory of kings.

I do pay attention to my dreams, and they showed me that a difficult, honey-less day like this was coming. So, as we sat at the restaurant, my dissociation tactics were in play as I floated away from our table and daydreamed of an easier time. But I couldn't escape entirely. The time did eventually come to leave the restaurant. My stomach is doing flips again just from writing about that day. This song lyric comes to mind to describe how I felt that day:

> There will be days your heart don't want to beat.
> You pray more than you breathe, and you just want to fall to
> pieces. [5]

An Agonizing Day, Continued

So we left the restaurant and stopped off at a friend's house to talk and pray. Then, off to walk the plank. I tried to think about other people who had been courageous like that paramedic who'd picked up God's Word in front of all those other paramedics, policemen, firemen and the fire chief and read it to me. I thought about people like Martin Luther King and Ruby Bridges and Jesus. Somehow it helped me to feel better thinking about how others had been brave when it was very difficult to be. I felt like, "If they can, I can."

We arrived intentionally a few minutes late as I wanted to arrive after all the others were there so we could start immediately. For the most part, the plan worked. Our pastor offered everyone coffee and water, and I just wanted to yell, "No, we don't need to chit chat and get drinks. Sit down, shut up, and let's get this over with!"

Eventually the drinks were dispersed, and the men were seated. I wished the earth would be gracious enough to open and swallow me whole. It was not. The few bites I'd taken at dinner were trying to defy gravity. I made them comply with the laws of physics, heavy stuff must stay down. I wished that was true emotionally as well.

My legs felt hollow and my stomach violent. My heart was apparently trying to pump all its blood into my ears because all I could hear was its activity. I think that someone opened us up with prayer, but I couldn't be certain. I was thirty-seven-years old and I felt every bit of six. Maybe that's because it was the little girl in me who would be speaking that night, sharing what she'd been through. I, or should I say "she," began to bear her soul before the church board. A couple of the men listening that night would go on to be loving and supportive. Some, turned against that little girl in a cruel and evil way and sided with her abuser.

Weak people don't like the truth because it sometimes makes life more difficult, more uncomfortable. There's a reason that victims of sexual crimes don't tell. I lived that reason. I have extremely thick skin and can be tough as nails, but I found people's hatred towards me in this process to be excruciating and unbearably painful. I can't imagine a little girl "telling" and experiencing the kind of fallout that accompanies this kind of honesty.

As it turns out, being 'courage on display' isn't for cowards.

Question 1: Do you need to do something that will require courage? God tells us all through Scripture, "Have courage!" "Don't be afraid!" "Take heart!" (See Deuteronomy 31:6, Joshua 1:6, Joshua 10:25, 1 Chronicles 28:20, Matthew 14:27, 1 Corinthians 16:13, Matthew 10:31, Mark 5:36, 2 Timothy 1:7.)

When He leads you to do something that will call for bravery, He will give you the strength to do it. It's in those difficult situations where we can learn how to borrow from His strength. He's offering it to you. So be brave. He's saying, "Here, have (My) courage, don't be afraid, take (My) heart." Be strong and courageous, and do not be afraid.

Question 2: Are there any dreams you've had more than once? Ask God to show you what He's been trying to tell you with those dreams.

*If you've ever had the courage to tell on someone evil and people turned against you when you told, I'm so sorry that happened to you. Shame on them! You are brave, and I'm proud of you for telling! They will give an account for their actions when they stand before God. Pity the fools.

Endnotes:

[1] Amos, Tori. Recorded 2012. Deutsche Grammophon, Mercury Classics.

[2] Timberlake, Justin, Chris Godbey, Timothy Mosely, Garland Mosely, James Fauntleroy, Jerome Harmon. "Drink You Away." Recorded 2015. RCA Nashville.

[3] John, Elton, Bernie Taupin, and Davey Johnston. "I Guess That's Why They Call it the Blues." Recorded 1982. Rocket.Rocket, 1982.

4 Leaf, Caroline, PhD. Who Switched Off My Brain? USA: Thomas Nelson, 2009.

[5] Copperman, Ross, and John Nite. "Break On Me." Recorded 2015. Capitol Nashville.

CHAPTER 18

The Fallout

There's a spirit of a storm in my soul.
A restlessness that I can't seem to tame.
The thunder and lightening follow everywhere I go.
There's a spirit of a storm in my soul.
There's a hurricane that's raging through my blood.
And I can't find a way to calm the sea.
Maybe I'll find someday the waters aren't so rough,
but right now they've got the best of me.
And oh, it's been a long, long time
since I had real peace of mind. [1]

Fall

I survived telling, *barely*. I survived that whole summer, *barely*. God, my husband, my counselor, and my pain management program got me through. The storm in my soul raged; morning, noon, and night. I welcomed fall with hopes of it being kinder.

The fall leaves usually send me into a reflective place, although, so do the winter branches, the summer sun, and the spring rains. This colorful, fall day as I sped down the tree-lined avenue in my Charcoal-tinted mini-van, I took in the spectrum of colors with much jubilation.

Falling leaves are so metaphorical, and God knows I'm a sucker for a good metaphor. Fall leaves also made me think of some of my favorite song lyrics. I'm a sucker for good song lyrics, too. Like Jackson Browne's song "Daddy's Tune" that says:

> *Well that dirty wind blows through the sky,*
> *and the autumn leaves cut loose and fly,*
> *leave me watchin' and wishin' I could follow.*[2]

Boy, could I relate to that song. If God would've allowed that dirty wind to take me right on up into the sky, I would've happily gone.

By fall, it'd been so long since I'd tasted wild honey. I wondered if my only shot at having it again was up in the clouds. I couldn't even remember where I'd put all the honey I'd jarred through the years. It seemed that wild honey was a thing of my past. Hardship, pain, and bitterness marked my days now.

Continuing with my fall playlist, I listened to The Eagle's "Wasted Time" lyrics:

> *The autumn leaves have got you thinking about the first time*
> *that you fell.*
> *You didn't love the boy too much.*
> *No, No, you just loved the boy too well.*
> *So you live from day to day and you dream about tomorrow.*
> *And the hours go by like minutes and the shadows come to stay,*
> *so you take a little something to make them go away.*
> *I could have done so many things, baby,*

if I could only stop my mind from wondering what I left behind,
and from worrying about this wasted time [3]

I almost never let my mind wonder about what I'd left behind. I tried not to think about all the wasted time I'd spent dealing with the mess that someone else had made in my life. So much of my life had been stolen. So much had been wasted. I rarely allowed myself to consider this for a variety of reasons. One reason was I was an eternal optimist. I had to be. I had to believe that things were forever going to get better than they'd been. That belief kept me from killing myself. I don't think that was wishful thinking though. In a lot of ways, things had gotten better through the years.

Another reason I didn't allow myself to think about wasted time was because those thoughts put me on a slippery slope. I walked a fine line where if I allowed myself the indulgence of feeling sorry for myself, I'd slip into the prison of depression. If I started to meditate on the way I'd been victimized, darkness would take over my mind with a rape-like force. (I guess I'm a sucker for a good pun as well.) I didn't normally think about my history of pain and sorrow as it was too painful and too sorrowful. I didn't like to feel that way, so I rarely, almost never, thought about it. My survival skills required me to look for happy things incessantly.

Feel It

Today, however, as I was still in the healing process, I contemplated the gross tragedies that had scarred my life and the long-term, ongoing consequences of them. This contemplation took my breath away, *literally*. I felt like I'd been punched in the gut and like that punch sent a tidal wave of pain throughout my body.

Wasted time, or rather, stolen time-today I thought about it.

I was 37 years old, and I was just now able to face the thief. I didn't want to face him. I didn't want to tell on him. I didn't want to think about him. But, for 60 to 90 seconds I allowed myself to step down off denial's platform and consciously consider what had been taken from me. It's enough to make you fall to your knees. I got so sad, and then I got so angry. I knew I had to let myself to *feel* what this man had done to me so I could gather up the fortitude needed to see the process through. Denial would never let me tell. Denial is a liar though, so be careful what kind of advice you take from her.

Counting The Cost

As I mentioned earlier, I did the best I could to count the cost of telling. I weighed out what it would cost me emotionally, physically, relationally, financially, and spiritually before I told. We should always count the cost before making a huge decision. This is the problem I ran into: There's no possible way to count the cost of something when there are a thousand different variables. There were so many aspects of my situation I couldn't possibly have anticipated.

After counting the cost as much as I possibly could, I chose to tell. Wisely, the church's senior pastor urged the elders to hire an attorney and third party private investigator to conduct a thorough investigation into the claims I brought forward. I was asked to assemble a list of other girls I thought might also have been victims of his. My mod did that for me and gave it over to the investigator.

The man who had abused me had been the college-age student

minister for a couple decades before he became the children's minister. While he was in that position, he dated any half-way decent looking girl that came through the ministry. That's right, while he was the *pastor* over the college group he dated most of the girls that were *students* in the college group! It's appalling he wasn't fired for that. But as far as I know, he wasn't even rebuked for it. Can you say "dysfunctional"?

Cowards Suck

So, there was a long list of girls that could be contacted. Most of the girls couldn't be found, but three of them that were found had been victims of his, showing a pattern of extremely immoral, sexual behavior while he was a pastor. Remember how "Being courage on display isn't for cowards"? Well, that's an unfortunate truth because all those other girls proved to be cowards! When it came time for them to share their truth with the investigator, they chickened out. They each had their reasons, I'm sure. But when you are stripped naked and laid bare before a governing board of men, other girls being cowards costs you greatly! Trust me on this one. I paid a heavy price because of those cowards.

I don't understand cowards. I really don't. I'm not a coward, by choice, not because it's easy. I *choose* to face my fears and attempt to overcome them. I believe any fear you don't face and overcome will master you. Fear gives birth to slaves. I know that having courage is difficult, but put on your big girl panties, and do difficult things! When it came right down to it, none of the other girls were brave enough to be honest. This made my nightmare even worse. Their shrinking back and letting fear and embarrassment guide them, made it look like I was the only one that had seen the dark side of this man. It made it *look* that way, but that was not the truth!

There were Scriptures I'd never understood until I went through this. Now I completely understand why God speaks so harshly to those who are cowardly. God loves truth and light. When you shrink back from telling the truth and, therefore, harbor sin safely in darkness, God is displeased. Take a look at how God feels about what these girls did:

Hebrews 10:38 *(NIV)*
*"But my righteous one will live by faith. And **I take no pleasure in the one who shrinks back.**"*

Hebrews 10:39 *(NIV)*
*But we do not belong to those who **shrink back** and are destroyed, but to those who have faith and are saved.*

Revelation 21:7-8 *(NIV)*
*Those who are victorious will inherit all this, and I will be their God and they will be my children. But the **cowardly**, the unbelieving, the vile, the murderers, the **sexually immoral**, those who practice magic arts, the idolaters and **all liars**— they will be consigned to the fiery lake of burning sulfur. This is the second death.*

God speaks in clear, strong language when it comes to being cowardly and lying. I get it-*now*. When I really needed these girls to step up in courage and speak, they shrunk back. Their actions heaped pain on my horrific situation! It also made the church board's job so much more difficult. Now they were mostly faced with a "he said, she said" situation instead of "all these girls say versus- he says" situation.

So, the investigator did his work, and *thank God,* still managed to conclude this man was guilty. My abuser was caught in his own lies at that point, at least for part of what he'd done.

At the end of the investigation I received the call from one of the elders saying this pastor who'd abused me was going to "resign." Because none of the other girls would talk, the board was told to let the pastor resign as opposed to him being fired. I was so angry with the other girls, but ultimately had to turn them over to God, and I already knew how He felt about their actions. Since all this ended, there have been several other girls who have also told me about things he did to them, though not one of them was willing to come forward publicly. They had heard what people were saying about me, and they didn't think they could handle those horrible things being said about them. Nice. Thanks.

Satan's Strategy

I guess it all makes sense though. If you're Satan and you've worked, manipulated, and maneuvered to get someone *who works for you* into a position of spiritual authority at a church, I'm sure you'd be working overtime to keep him there. By my telling on this man, I was exposing a satanic strategy that had been in place and operating undetected for several *decades*. I'm sure Satan was furious with me. If you don't think that is a satanic strategy to get pastors to stay on staff at a church while they molest children and sleep with college students, then whose strategy is it?

Satan's three main schemes are: Try to get us to work for him, to take us out, or at the very least neutralize us. As long as we are completely ineffective for the Kingdom of God, he wins on some level. But, when we consider that there is a satanic strategy, we shouldn't be surprised by the evil we see happening in our churches, let alone in the world.

Time For The Church To Know

So, this pastor would resign instead of be fired, and it would be announced this Sunday. Sunday arrived and finally the church was going to be informed about the results of the investigation. This man had been found guilty and would be stepping down. I knew the church would be surprised, but thought once they heard the investigator had concluded this man was guilty, they would understand. Unfortunately, that was not how it went.

I requested that one of the elders in particular *not* be the one to make the announcement because he was a close friend and open supporter of my abuser and critic of me. Plainly, I didn't want him to make the announcement because he is a wolf. My husband called one of the other elders and requested one thing, please don't let that man make the announcement. To our shock he *was* the one who made the announcement! He began to speak in a solemn, sad tone. Unfortunately, his sadness was on behalf of the child molester, not the child.

"Two weeks ago I informed the congregation on behalf of the eldership that our associate minister "Pastor Chuck" had been placed on paid administrative leave pending an investigation in a recent complaint made about *alleged* conduct that occurred *over twenty years ago.* The primary allegations involved alleged sexual misconduct, *again over twenty years ago.* Nevertheless, the eldership took these allegations very seriously and initiated an immediate investigation. A thorough investigation was performed by a trained and experienced outside investigator. "Pastor Chuck" fully cooperated in the investigation and met with the investigator on multiple occasions as we requested. "Pastor Chuck" *strongly* denies the alleged sexual misconduct and continues to do so. There are no direct witnesses to the alleged sexual misconduct. For a variety reasons, based on the investigation that was reviewed by the eldership in multiple meetings, and after much deliberation the eldership has concluded the evidence of alleged sexual misconduct against "Pastor Chuck" was *inconclusive*. Given the entire situation "Pastor Chuck" has decided to resign. In recognition of his many years of service to the congregation, the eldership has offered a severance package that includes his full pay and benefits for one year while "Pastor Chuck" transitions to another place of employment.

"It is very important that you keep everyone involved in your prayers. We need to show love and support to everyone involved, and we will do so. We're a family of God and we can deal with this and continue on with the many works we are called to do as a church. The eldership asks that you refrain from speculation, rumors, and gossip that would serve no purpose other than to damage others, and it really isn't the Christian way. We ask that you show love and respect to everyone involved regardless of what you may feel about the outcome. The elders love and welcome all involved and want to do everything possible to begin a time of healing and restoration and are ready to do whatever is necessary to further the goal, this goal with much prayer and with faith, and we ask you all to do the same."

Perhaps this statement doesn't look as bad as it felt. I don't know. I can't be objective about this. The main complaint I had was that the statement was a lie and was more honoring to the abuser than to the victim! They said the investigation was "inconclusive." I had been told in no uncertain terms that the investigator concluded that "Chuck" was guilty and that he'd been caught in a lie! Also, in the statement made to the church they said he adamantly denied everything, but that wasn't true either. He'd admitted to *part* of what he had done. They couldn't legally allow a man who admitted to doing what he'd done to continue in a pastoral role, but that's not what they told the church.

So why did this man say to the church that the investigation was inconclusive? I managed to find humor in the fact that they said that there were no witnesses. How often are there witnesses to molestation and rape? By the elders forcing this pastor to resign, but acting like he was choosing to resign because he's a good guy they made *him* look like the victim. By presenting things in such a way as to say, "We've found nothing here, but in light of everything he's resigning," it makes him sound like a hero that was a victim to false accusations.

By the elders presenting things the way that they did, it caused the church to rally behind *him*. By the other girls not sharing what he'd done to them, it caused me to look like a lone victim and, therefore, a potential liar. After that, my abuser, the pastor did not leave the church immediately. You would think after all this, he'd leave the church in a hurry, but he stayed around the church for a few more weeks to try to get a message out that would defend his reputation. He went to each adult Sunday school class defending himself to each group, playing the victim, and maligning me. He's an extremely controlling and manipulative man. Plainly, he's an excellent liar. I, therefore, became a despised woman.

Couldn't Count On That One

So, when I counted the cost, I couldn't have counted on these variables going the way that they did. I was the victim of a pastor who had manipulated, controlled, abused, and raped me for years in my pre-teen and teenager years, and now I was being re-victimized by a number of people from my church who chose to stand with him, against me. Think that one through for a moment. A pastor has sex with a little girl and then when she tells, people side with *him*. I imagined what their conversations were like at home. "Well, the pastor never had sex with *me*, so that girl must by lying." Honestly, I don't know what these people talked about, or how they justified that man, and themselves. I look forward to the day each of these people stand before God and find out that they stood by and defended a lying, perverse, evil, child-molester.

Some of the church leaders told my husband and me they were glad we didn't come back to church after I told on the pastor because they were afraid people at the church would have formed a lynch mob against us. The victim of childhood sexual assaults was being told that "the crowd" appears to be supporting the perpetrator, not you. Wrap your brain around that one for a moment! If there's not something so dark and backwards about that, then I don't know what's what; yet, that's what happens most of the time in these kinds of cases! What was even more bizarre to me was that people who were "on his side" never even heard my side! They only heard his loud, lying side. They never took the time to consider there was another side to that story that just wasn't so loud.

So few people seemed to care about the truth. There were close friends who I'd obviously told about what had happened, but apart from close friends, most people never even knew the facts. They just blindly took his side. While the abuser (or "the rapist," as my husband refers to him as), was out talking to anyone who would listen, I was silent. I had no voice. I was un-friended by many church members and church leaders on Facebook. I was unfriended by several of the elders and their wives, and I unfriended some who I heard were slandering and opposing me. Not one of those people heard my side of it. My only police was the fact that God knew the truth and that truth has a way of coming out. Also, when God said He would be my defender, I chose to believe Him.

Re-victimizing the Victim

I saw "Christians" act nothing like Christ. I heard I was being gossiped about and maligned. In one of the books I read during my healing process it says that often the victim of sexual crimes is more villainized than the perpetrator. When I read this, I hadn't yet told what this man had done to me, so it wasn't my reality yet. I read it with much naivety, wondering how that could *possibly* be true. Now I understand its truth. I heard from people that I, the victim, was hated because I'd destroyed a "good man's life." I wish they could see how "good" he was while he was raping me.

I think we must ask ourselves why we do this? Why do we turn against the girls who say they've been molested or raped? Why can't we handle the truth? Why does accepting a difficult reality scare us so badly that we will actually deny the reality so that we can remain comfortable? We need to ask ourselves why our first question tends to be, "I wonder what she did or wore to tempt him?" Or we just completely dismiss the allegations, assuming she's probably lying. The main question I'd love for us to ask ourselves is "What does this girl gain by saying that she was raped?" Let me answer that question for you. In most cases she gains insults, ridicule, hatred, mockery, being lied about, judged, scorned, and shunned-especially by the church. So, why would a girl lie about this kind of thing? "Telling" nearly ruined my life. If you think most girls would lie about this kind of thing, you're being unintelligent. Someone who was insane might lie about this, but the percentage of people who lie is hardly worth mentioning.

Most in the church *wanted* to believe the pastor wouldn't do something like this, so they did. They had not seen the dark side of this man, so they assumed that side must not exist. It is disappointing to me how few people can discern the truth from a lie. But I saw something much more concerning than people not discerning truth from lie. I saw that many people don't even *WANT* to know the truth. When the truth disrupts their comfort level or long-held beliefs, often they don't want to know it. Their desire for comfort and security trumps their desire for truth. What a tragic and cowardice desire.

In Conclusion

Although, I did have more courage than those other girls, I was also experiencing more repercussions than they were. I perceived that their repercussions were feeling a little guilty that they'd hung me out to dry. My repercussions were life-altering, exposing, scarring, and humiliating. They seemed to float on through their lives while I was busy picking up the pieces that were created by this humiliating hurricane that came through mine. I was made a public spectacle and was wearing the scarlet letter. They weren't. They were hiding in shadows, but they weren't being emotionally whipped and berated. Maybe I was the fool after all.

As I was picking up the pieces of my life, I wondered if the cost of courage was too high a price to pay. It felt like my reputation and life would never recover. The loss was significant, the pain intolerable. Maybe I shouldn't have told. Maybe I should have taken the same route his other victims took. I mean, how big a deal is it to let a perverse, child-molesting, rapist stay in the position of children's pastor anyway?

Question: Have you ever been a coward and let someone else pay the price while you looked out for yourself? On the flip-side, have you ever paid a high price to be brave? Have you ever judged someone who said she'd been sexually abused, rather than show-ing her compassion? Did it ever occur to you that people who "tell" have nothing to gain by telling? Is there anyone you need to apologize to? Don't allow yourself just to feel bad about it; find her and apologize.

Endnotes:

1 Chesney, Kenny, and Brett James. "Spirit of a Storm." Recorded 2008. Blue Chair Records/BNA.

2 Browne, Jackson. "Daddy's Tune" Recorded 1976. Asylum/Elektra.

3 The Eagles. "Wasted Time" Recorded 1976. Asylum.

CHAPTER 19

"317"

*Bad things do happen; how I respond to them defines my
character and the quality of my life. I can choose to sit in
perpetual sadness, immobilized by the gravity of my loss, or I
can choose to rise from the pain and treasure the most precious
gift I have–life itself.* [1]

In those days that followed telling on my main abuser, I felt
a cavernous ache in my belly, and a heaviness in my spirit. The
heaviness wasn't contained to my spirit; it was felt all over my
body. My legs felt dense. Every step was fatiguing. I felt like I
had a thick, weighted blanket draped over my shoulders. Perhaps I felt all that physical weight because emotional pain causes physical pain. Or perhaps it was because I was medicating
myself with food. Apparently the "eat and drink whatever you
want, whenever you want" philosophy didn't work well for me.
None of my clothes were fitting anymore.

Almost every time I left my house, I would run into someone from the church that would either walk away when she saw me or would be flat out rude to my face. It felt like the enemy set up an endless number of mean encouters for me. Indeed, I think he had. It was bad. I began feeling paranoid, seeing hermit-like tendencies in myself. I just wanted to stay in my closet... all day. Many days I did just that; I literally stayed in my closet. At times the light of day was too painful for my eyes. My kids would come in and visit me in my closet. I'd put a towel across the bottom of the closet door so there would be absolutely no light at all. I'd take the pillows from my bed into the closet, and we'd lay on our backs just talking or listening to music. We had some of the sweetest conversations in that dark closet floor. We still talk about those memories fondly. I know how bizarre that is, But even in all this, God provided wonderful times with my children we will never forget!

Based on how the people from this church were treating me, it felt like few believed me. I have no clue what the actual numbers were, but only a handful of people (four in all) reached out to me and showed me the love of Christ. I felt so rejected. No, I WAS so rejected.

It seemed like I was even an embarrassment to my friends. I noticed my "friends" did not "like" or comment on my Facebook posts. I'd see they "liked" and commented on other people's stuff; but when I posted, it was like I had the plague. I think people didn't want to be seen publicly associating with me. So many people were against me, and they knew associating with me would cause them to be alienated by my adversaries. Apparently, they wanted to be a relational "Switzerland" and try to make everyone happy. So they'd say privately that we were still friends, but publicly had nothing to do with me. I've grown to despise Switzerland.

It got to a point where I was begging God to let me move out of my city. I prayed every day that a way would be made for my family to move far, far away from this place. I couldn't imagine how I could ever live here and move about freely after all the hurtful things that had happened to me. For example, on Christmas day my family had gone to see a movie, and we saw a couple from this church walking up to the theater. When the wife spotted us, she said to her husband, "Ugh, there are the Hamms and the Roberts! Let's walk over that way," and she pointed to taking the long way around so she wouldn't have to walk near us. We could *hear* her saying that.

Another time I was on a field trip with our youngest son. As I approached the group I was with, I saw the wife of one of the elders. She was staring at me with her mouth hanging open, as if she was watching a freak show. When I turned to look her in her eyes, she just quickly turned away. Then, only a few minutes later another elderly couple from the church was walking towards my son and me. I'd seen them, but they hadn't seen me. I thought at least they'd probably be kind, since they were older and, therefore, more mature. Instead, the wife grabbed her husband's arm, gasped, and said, "There's Rachel Hamm! Go that way," as she pointed towards walking the other way.

Rejection. I've experienced scorn and rejection on a level most never will. I felt like there was no one on earth who understood what kind of torment I was experiencing at that time and like I had experienced in my childhood. It was like I had leprosy. I had become the community leper.

So, I did what I'd done my whole life. I took that hate to Jesus and asked Him to vindicate me. I asked Him to comfort and heal me. I was very intentional about what I allowed myself to think during this time and constantly asked the Lord, "What do

You say about me?" In order to survive during that time, I had to learn to live for the approval of God and God alone. That had to be enough for me. I'm so thankful I learned that lesson. After all, living for God's approval alone is the best way to live.

Another dynamic going on at that time was that I feared for my life. My main abuser always told me he'd kill me if I told on him. He and his wife told me on multiple occasions how many guns and how much ammunition they owned. Once I told, I lived with the sense I could be murdered at any time. I was always looking out my window and watching for anyone coming to my door. I had to learn how to be led of God regarding when to leave my house and where to go and not go. I learned how to be so tuned into the Holy Spirit that I could receive instruction for every turn I made. I'm thankful I learned that lesson, too. That's a powerful way to live. Not being afraid, being led minute-by-minute by the Holy Spirit.

Bad Guys

One day a godly woman who I respect and who hears from the Lord told me she'd been praying for me and while she was praying, the Lord told her to give me a warning. This woman has a ministry helping people who have been connected to satanic groups and are now seeking freedom. Because of that she knows about the tactics they use. God showed her a man would be coming to my front dor, probably in a uniform of some sort, who was actually being sent from a satanic coven to curse me. She told me he would want to give me some sort of object that was cursed. He'd want me to take it from him so the cursed object would be brought in to affect the atmosphere of my home.

All the blood drained from my face as this woman spoke.

"What's wrong?" she asked. "Did this already happen?"

"Yes, yesterday!" I said. I went on to tell her how a man had come to my house and immediately I sensed something wasn't right! You know that little twinge in your gut that says, "Somethings off!"? I had that. So much so that I wouldn't open my door for him, which is not like me. My dog was standing at the door growling at whoever this was, and she never growls.

The man was in a uniform, and he said he was sent to me from my insurance company to measure each room of the house. I said we didn't own this house and he'd need to talk to the owner to do anything like that. He persisted saying it wouldn't take long, and our policy might lapse if he didn't come in and measure. Knowing something didn't feel right, I did not let him in. He finally resigned his request to this, "Well, just let me measure around the outside of the house then. That might be good enough. I'd also need to get on the roof, but then that should be good enough."

Not being far enough along in my healing process to have the strength to say, "NO!" I gave into this last request. Prior to healing, I struggled with wanting to please people. I did not want him to measure the outside of my house, nor get on my roof, but I didn't have the emotional strength to stick to my guns and make him leave. I felt so uneasy and all my internal, gut-level alarms were going off. I went around and locked all my doors. Later, I'd learn that locked doors don't protect you from evil. God alone can do that.

After he'd "measured" he came back to the front door and wanted to give me some papers. I cracked open the door with my dog in front of me. He slid his papers through the crack. Unfortunately, it only takes a cracked door for the enemy to make his way in.

Finally, he left. Now, however, listening to this woman who heard God's warning, I felt so uneasy. I knew my gut had been right, and he was a "bad guy." This woman suggested maybe he was legit, and I should call my landlord to see if someone from his insurance company was supposed to come to measure. I called. The landlord said, "No! I'd *never* allow someone to come measure the house without telling you first, and they'd never just show up on your doorstep. I didn't get a new policy. There's no need for anyone to have been measuring anything. I don't know who it was that came to your door, but I hope you didn't let him in!"

My heart sank. A satanic, coven-loyal, bad guy had just been to my home, touching every square inch of my house, and had been on my roof. This is classic coven work. They want to touch, and therefore place a curse on, as much as possible. Think of it as the same concept as God saying to His people, "I will give you every place you set your foot." Only the kingdom of darkness is using this strategy for its purpose. People operating in darkness, meaning people who are cooperating and being led by Satan, often understand how blessing and cursing works better than Christ followers.

In this season when I was waging war on the dark, wounded places in my own self, there were at least four times (that I'm aware of) that a satanic person came to my house. One even came to my house and killed a raven in my yard. Coven people completely understand the power of a blood sacrifice! I wish believers in Christ would have a better understanding of that! Christ followers have access to the highest level of blood sacrifice of all time, the blood of Jesus.

I know you might not have any clue what I even mean when I say, "There were at least four times (that I'm aware of) that a satanic person came to my house." You might not be aware of satanic covens, what they do, or how they operate. This isn't the place to explain all that. But know this: there really is an enemy of God, and he really does have people currently working for him. They're attempting to sabotage anything or anyone operating in the Kingdom of Light. I have the unfortunate privilege of knowing about this, firsthand.

If your church is making a difference and being a light to your community then there are satanic people assigned to your church. They are sent in as wolves amongst the sheep. They are assigned to cause dissension, to try to get the leaders to become prideful, and wound or deceive the sheep. If they can't get your leaders to become prideful they'll send someone seductive to try to move them into sexual sin. They also try to worm their way into leadership positions within your church. Ultimately, they want to malign the name of Jesus and lead people away from Him. I understand that you might have a hard time believing that, but this is happening whether you believe it or not. This is what Jesus says to us:

Behold, I am sending you out as sheep in the midst of wolves, so be wise as serpents and innocent as doves.
(Matthew 10:16, ESV)

Don't let this information cause you to be fearful. If you belong to Christ, then greater is He that is in you than he who is in the world. You have more authority through the Name of Jesus than any satanic person has. You can pray. You can be wise. If God is with you, who can be against you?

I am fully aware that I will probably be criticized for putting this information out there. Some might think I'm crazy. If satanic people hear about this they will try to discredit me, *obviously.* They don't want their activity exposed. I know that I am taking a risk by exposing this reality. But for those who have an ear to hear...remember that you can tell what kind of tree a tree is based on what kind of fruit its producing. If a sheep is acting like it's a wolf, be wise.

Knowing that satanic people were coming to my house, I thought, "If my neighbors knew they lived next to someone who might be murdered at any given moment, and who has satanists coming to her house, they'd want me to move out of the neighborhood." I never told a neighbor about any of it because I couldn't handle any more rejection at that point. The church already had that covered. The anguish was too intense without my neighbors adding to it.

Where Does My Help Come From?

I had to learn to trust that my days were in God's hands. Hearing that and believing that are two different things. I asked for God's protection all the time. I remember one day when I was afraid I was going to be killed, I turned on Daystar Christian Television to find some comfort, some hope. I was amazed as I listened to John Hagee speak of a near-death experience that day. He said a man walked into where he was speaking and held up a gun and shot at him. Pastor Hagee held up his Bible in front of him and said, "In the name of Jesus, you will not be able to kill me. My days are in God's hands." I listened to him tell this story and *knew* God was showing me *He* was my protector. That man's bullets went to the right and to the left, but never hit pastor Hagee. I borrowed courage from that.

During these desolate days, I also began having the strangest thing happen. I began seeing the number 317 *EVERYWHERE*. For example, it seemed like I looked at the clock only two times in a 24-hour period: 3:17 AM and 3:17 PM. I'd be driving down the street and pull up behind a car that had a license plate that would be P317317. Someone would give me an address, and it would be 317 W. Jones Street. I'd have to enter the 3-digit security code on the back of my credit card, and it would be 317. Everywhere, and I mean *everywhere*, I saw the number 317.

I didn't have the faintest clue why that was happening, and it started to bug me. Finally, one day when I'd seen 317 four times all within just a few hours, I realized God *might* be telling me something. So, I prayed, "God, WHY ON EARTH AM I SEEING 317? Are YOU telling me something? What is 317?"

I heard in my spirit, "Open your Bible to Psalms 31:7 and begin reading." This is what it said:

7- I will be glad and rejoice in your love,
for you saw my affliction
and knew the anguish of my soul.
8-You have not given me into the hands of the enemy
but have set my feet in a spacious place.

9-Be merciful to me, Lord, for I am in distress;
my eyes grow weak with sorrow,
my soul and body with grief.

10-My life is consumed by anguish
and my years by groaning;
my strength fails because of my affliction,
and my bones grow weak.
11-Because of all my enemies,
I am the utter contempt of my neighbors
and an object of dread to my closest friends—
those who see me on the street flee from me.

12-I am forgotten as though I were dead;
I have become like broken pottery.

13-For I hear many whispering,

"Terror on every side!"
They conspire against me
and plot to take my life.

♪.

14-But I trust in you, Lord;
I say, "You are my God."
15-My times are in your hands;
deliver me from the hands of my enemies,
from those who pursue me.

16-Let your face shine on your servant;
save me in your unfailing love.
17-Let me not be put to shame, Lord,
for I have cried out to you;
but let the wicked be put to shame
and be silent in the realm of the dead.
18-Let their lying lips be silenced,
for with pride and contempt
they speak arrogantly against the righteous.

19-How abundant are the good things
that you have stored up for those who fear you,
that you bestow in the sight of all,
on those who take refuge in you.

20-In the shelter of your presence you hide them
from all human intrigues;
you keep them safe in your dwelling
from accusing tongues.

21-Praise be to the Lord,
for he showed me the wonders of his love
when I was in a city under siege.

22-In my alarm I said,
"I am cut off from your sight!"
Yet you heard my cry for mercy
when I called to you for help.

23-Love the Lord, all his faithful people!
The Lord preserves those who are true to him,

but the proud he pays back in full.

24-Be strong and take heart,
all you who hope in the Lord.

I cried and cried *and cried* as I read. God knew! He knew and saw and cared about my anguish. Through these Scriptures, God showed me He knew every single thing I was feeling and experiencing, and that I could call on His Name to be saved. David's words in this Psalm were virtually the exact expression of my heart! It was as if this Psalm had been written by me. The comfort I got from this passage was miraculous. David's God-inspired words were a healing balm for my soul.

After God led me to this passage in such a bizarre way I *knew* (*yet again*) that He was with me! I was strong, and I did take heart, because I put my full hope in the Lord. Sometimes the way God speak to us is so unusual in our way of thinking.

To this day I see 317 everywhere, and each time it serves as a reminder that God sees me and knows the deepest, most inward parts of me. He saw every person that had been hateful to me. He saw how people stopped commenting on my Facebook posts so they wouldn't be associated with me in any way. To be fully seen and known and understood is a very satisfying state to be in. I think we all have a deep-seated desire to be fully known, and still be fully accepted. He let me know I was not alone in my loneliness. That's God.

Even when people fail us, God never does. As I progressed through the healing process, He revealed to me a deeper understanding of His perfect nature. The further I got into the process of counseling and healing and understanding who God is I thought, "It's worth it. The pain, the rejection, the process, it's beginning to feel like it's worth it." Each month that passed I could look back and see the progress I'd made that month. Minute by minute, session by session, day by day, I was being healed and freed. I was also growing even deeper in my understanding of just how sweet our Healer is!

These song lyrics by Kenny Chesney summed up what I began to feel as my healing process got further along:

> *I ain't ever going back again.*
> *I'm feelin' comfortable in my skin.*
> *A little numb, but I'm on the mend.*
> *Yeah, I think I'm going to be OK...*
> *I ain't ever going back again.* [2]

God was obviously leading me to Psalm 31 because I needed it, no doubt. However, I think *the way* that He led me to it was for a different reason. I have asked God to give me holy adventure. I love excitement, and in my late teens, early 20s I thought, "My desire for adventure could really get me into trouble if I don't submit that desire to the Lord." So, again, *I asked!* I said, "God, if you don't give me some wild, holy adventure, I'm afraid that I'll make some bad decisions to get it. So, please make my life exciting! I really don't want to be bored!"

I think that request that I've made for years is part of why He does things like show me 317 everywhere; and why He put $20 in my pocket five days in a row. He does creative, fun, exciting things in my life. He could have just put it on my heart to read that Psalm, but instead He led me to it in a fun and creative way. That's why I've found walking with God to be such a blast. I don't get bored *because of God.*

Remember, Proverbs 25:2 says,

It is the glory of God to conceal a matter;
to search out a matter is the glory of kings.

There was still one more 317 surprise waiting for me. I didn't find it until I wrote the final words of this book...

Question: Have you ever experienced any "strange coincidences" that might have actually been God showing you something? Ask God to show you if there's anything you've missed. Need some wholesome excitement? Ask God for that, too!

Endnotes:

1 Walter Anderson, Accessed March 31, 2017. https://www.brainyquote.com/quotes/authors/w/walter_anderson.html.

2 Chesney, Kenny and James Brett. "I Ain't Ever Going Back Again." Recorded 2010. BNA.

CHAPTER 20

Paint By Numbers

And we'll fill in the missing colors
In each other's paint-by-numbers dreams [1]

There'd been a lot of dots on my page that I could never quite connect in order to create my paint-by-numbers life picture. Rather than a series of numbers that flowed in numerical order, mine seemed like random, nonsensical dots that were aimlessly dotted all over my life's canvas, never forming a pretty, completed picture. However, once I began remembering my full past and began to heal, an amazing thing happened! The dots began to connect! So many things in my life made sense for the first time, and that felt amazing! As I said before, "It was the best of times, it was the worst of times," and it never felt truer.

During counseling sessions, we would talk through different memories or flashbacks and as we did, different parts of me would appear and talk. In other words, the part of me created to deal with the trauma we were currently discussing would rise up and share information about what happened. Things would come out of me I had not consciously thought of since the event had happened.

It was a wild journey, *to say the least!* It was shocking how much had been locked away inside of me. But once we took the lid off, the flow of information began. And once it did, those dots began to take on numbers, and guess what? They were in numerical order! It felt like my life went from black and white to a full color scale with brilliant hues.

One of those random dots that never made sense to me was when my girlfriend asked me if that pastor had ever molested me. She'd asked me about two years prior to my having full memory of it. When she asked me, I'd said "No. Why?" She seemed genuinely shocked, which seemed strange to me at the time. It felt like she knew something about me I didn't even know about myself. Once I began counseling, I remembered she'd asked me that, and I called her and asked if we could meet.

She worked at a bank near a girly restaurant, so we made plans to meet on her lunch hour. As soon as we'd ordered, I turned to her and asked her if she remembered that conversation two years ago. She said yes, and I asked her *why* she had asked me that. She said, "I was sure that he had an inappropriate relationship with you. I was molested, so I tend to discern when that's happening to other people."

Ironically, this friend had dated this pastor. She was about ten years older than I was, and he was about six years older than she. She continued to tell me about how he had gotten very "physical" with her, very fast. He did this while he was the college ministries *pastor* and she was a *student* in that ministry.

I found out he had other inappropriate relationships with girls over 18, and she said there were signs that he'd molested me (a child). Then she said something I would go on to hear from many other people as the situation became public: "There didn't appear to be any other kids that he was weird with. It was clear that he was obsessed with *you!*"

I then asked her if he'd taken her out of town. He'd taken me out of town, and I knew he'd taken most of the girls he'd dated out of town, which begs the question: why didn't the church fire him on the spot? This church had a history of allowing sin to thrive and then be swept under the rug. She said, "He had planned a trip to take me out of town, but I got into a car accident the day we were supposed to go. I was so relieved so that I didn't have to go out of town with him. That's when I knew I needed to break up with him. When getting into a car accident is better than having to be alone with someone, something's wrong! Now I can see getting into that car accident was God's way of protecting me!"

"God's way of protecting me?" I thought. How could she say that to *me* when she knew something bad *did* happen to me? He *did* take me out of town. She was clearly not thinking about how her statement would make me feel. I just tried to shake off the insensitive comment for the time being.

Good Theology?

The next morning I was showering and praying. I told God what she'd said to me and that it appeared to me to be bad theology, but I didn't know for sure. Did He protect her, but not me? This pastor *had* taken me out of town and had sex with me. Why didn't God stop *that*? Why did she get into a car accident and cancel her trip, but my trip went uncanceled?

God did *not* answer my questions the way I expected, but instead He said, "Do you want *your* theology?"

I answered, "YES! I want to know the *truth!*"

He proceeded, not with words, but onto giving me another vision. I haven't had many visions in my life; but while I was in the counseling/healing process, I had a ton of them! This was the vision:

I saw myself lying in the Tahoe hotel room bed where this pastor had taken me. The pastor was on top of me. Then suddenly out of the wall I see Jesus, storming in with a whole host of angels following. Jesus' hands are held in front of Him in the sort of position that looked like He was going to choke someone. He had a furious look on His face, and He was glaring at the pastor as He charged in. I thought, "Oh man, this pastor is in serious trouble!" But to my surprise He passed by the pastor's head and went down to me.

His face softened and He cupped my face in His hands. He whispered into my ear, "Hurry, precious one, go on," as He motioned for me to go over to the corner of the room. I then saw my body float up and over to the corner where there was a huge angel holding his arms open to embrae me once I got to him.

But, what I saw next was disturbingly magnificent! I saw Jesus slide *Himself* underneath the pastor where I had been in the bed! I reached the angel, and he grabbed and held me against his muscly chest and wrapped his arms around me to hold and hide me. Up above us there were angels in a circle all around the ceiling of the room, and they were screaming, not saying, *screaming* *"MERCY! MERCY! MERCY! MERCY!"* I could hear no other sounds, only their cries of mercy being screamed as Jesus was being raped.

The vision ended and I sobbed as I slid by trembling body down the shower wall! Then, Jesus said to me, "I don't think people understand what I mean when I say that 'I take their shame.' I mean I *LITERALLY* TAKE IT! You know how you're remembering what happened, but it still feels like it happened to someone else? That's because it *did* happen to Someone Else. Someday that pastor will have to stand before Me and explain why he raped *Me*. *That's* your theology!"

> *"Truly, I say to you, as you did it to one of the least of these my*
> *brothers, you did it to ME."*
> *(Matthew 25:40, ESV)*

I sat shaking and weeping in the shower for awhile. What other religion has a God like the God of the Bible? What other religion has a Savior that comes and "literally takes our shame"? How can such a traumatic event be reframed and healed so powerfully apart from Jesus? It cannot. You can receive a partial healing apart from Jesus. But if you want to completely rewire a memory in a way that not only heals you but causes you to see redemption, that takes Jesus.

Question: Would you be willing to ask Jesus to give you visions? Visions can be powerfully healing to our souls. Ask Him.

Endnote:

[1] Browne, Jackson. "The Pretender" Recorded 1976. Asylum/Elektra.

CHAPTER 21

Thanks For The Invite!

Nobody said it was easy
It's such a shame for us to part
Nobody said it was easy
No one ever said it would be this hard [1]

Every summer my grandma (the one who gave me the white leather hot pants and brown, peach, and gold sweatshirt), would take our whole family to the beach for a week. She'd rent a big beach house right on the ocean. We'd all crowd in and enjoy the view and the company (mostly). My grandpa died before I was born, so it was just my grandma. Those she invited included my parents, brother and I, my mom's brother's family, and her sister's family. There were seven adults and seven grandchildren, with an occasional second cousin thrown in here and there.

Every year I looked forward to this week with sweet anticipation. It was a magical time. It was the only time I saw my mom's sister's family. In her family were three of my cousins, and there's just something about cousins, especially older ones. My mom's sister's family lived in other states, moving so much I couldn't keep track. My uncle was a basketball coach, and they moved often as better jobs opened up to him. So this week at the beach was my chance to get to know people I shared blood with, but little else. I would count down the days until this special week.

One day when I was about 12 my mom, brother, and I had gone to visit the grumpy grandma. While we were there, I asked my grandma which beach town we'd be staying in that year. She'd always relished picking different beach towns for us to explore all along the California coast. She hemmed and hawed, and didn't want to answer. Then, it dawned on me, she couldn't afford to do it this year!

I knew all about not being able to afford something! That was the story of my life. Not having enough money for our needs, let alone our wants, was humiliating! Grandma had been mentioning her costly medical bills, so I put two and two together–*she can't afford it*. Being as proud as she was, I knew she must be humiliated by this, so I tried to graciously let her off the hook. "Oh, have you decided not to get a house this year because of everyone's busy schedules?" I asked.

My grandma looked at my mom as if to say, "You tell her." My mom stared back as if to say "Nope." I looked between the two ladies to see which was going to tell me. They're both stubborn as mules, so it took a couple of minutes. I finally said "JUST TELL ME! What's going on?!"

My mom broke their silence just long enough to volley a question that forced my grandmother into admission. "Mom, are *you* going to the beach this year?" I turned to my grandmother, my forehead wrinkled with confusion. I waited. My grandma started breathing faster. This made me uneasy, as she was already hooked up to the strongest oxygen tank possible to assist her tar-filled lungs with one simple task, breathing successfully. Grandma looked away from me and stared out her gigantic picture windows. Her eyes were darting nervously between the Liquid Amber Maple trees that graced her 1950s backyard.

She was able to calm her brain and her lungs enough to explain, "*I am* going to the beach this year."

"By yourself?" I asked.

"No." She answered. We sat staring at each other in silence. Good grief, just say it already! Why was she acting so weird?

"So we *are* going to the beach?" I asked as I continued to seek clarification. Her delay in responding seemed so odd. Finally, "Your Aunt Anne, Uncle Lynn, and their kids, Uncle Joe, and Aunt Karen, and their kids, and your mom's cousin Roxi, and I are going."

"OH! Good, we *are* going! You were acting so weird that I thought we weren't going or something."

My mom spoke up again only to say one word, "*Mom!*"

My grandma nearly leapt when my mom called her name. "No, *we're* not going, Rachel. *You're* not going." I was starting to get it, and I was starting to get mad!

"So, *we're* not invited? Don't *you* do the inviting? *You* didn't invite us, Grandma?" I now felt no desire to be gracious or let her off the hook in any way, anymore. My blood was boiling and my feelings were hurt.

My mom's brother and my dad had some relational problems that had led to some business problems, or the other way around;

I'm not sure which came first. Just prior to this conversation with my grandma, my dad and uncle discontinued doing business together. Apparently, in my grandmother's eyes, we could no longer vacation together either.

It's all fun and games until grandma pokes your eye out!

I don't really remember the rest of that conversation. I just remember how it made me feel: rejected. That wasn't just a feeling, my family *was* being rejected. I guess it's true you don't usually remember what people say, you remember how they make you feel. It seemed like she didn't think we could vacation together, so she had to pick and she picked THEM, and NOT ME.

I don't think there's a more demoralizing experience than rejection, especially when it comes at the hands of your own family. Her choice, her rejection meant I would never see any of my cousins again as a child. This parting of ways also meant holidays where we would normally be with my grandma and my in-town uncle, aunt, and cousins would now be spent alone. Thanksgiving seems strange when it's just you, your brother, and parents. And summers without a week at the beach was such a sad loss to me. I wondered why I was so easy to walk away from. I would have fought tooth and nail to continue to see my cousins and to have relationships with them. Why weren't they fighting to see me? I knew it was because I wasn't worth the fight.

As always, my parents tried to point out the positives. We'd never have to spend another Thanksgiving listening to "grumpy grandma" complain about our incorrect grammar or our bad table manners. Not being around our little cousins would be nice, they said, but it really wasn't true. We were so sad and felt the sting of rejection. Holidays emphasized the magnitude of our loss and our feelings of being unwanted. Ultimately, I discovered that hidden in that loss was also an invitation.

Through the pain of that rejection, I was invited to value people's character rather than their titles. It doesn't matter if your title is "Grandma" if you reject your own family. It doesn't matter if your title is "Uncle" if your lack of character prevents you from filling that role. It doesn't matter if your title is "pastor"; what matters is your character. I also learned sharing blood is not that important when your blood lines are screwed up! I learned that God's family is stronger than a biological family. Family is not defined by shared blood. Family is defined as relationships that stand the test of time, fire, and trial. My extended family rejecting me gave me an invitation to learn some life lessons. I accepted the invitation to learn these things and became better for it.

My parents didn't seem to feel rejected. They seemed relieved because they knew what I didn't know: one of our relatives was involved in some inappropriate activities. From where I stood as a kid, my perspective said I'd been rejected. From where God and my parents stood, we'd just been delivered. Sometimes we can't see the full reality of something because of our limited perspective at the time. Over time, my pain lessened, and I learned to adjust to my new family-less way of celebrating holidays.

We were very involved in our church and those relationships helped fill the gaps. We had lots of friends and were surrounded by people who *did* want to be around us. That eased the pain of our family's rejecting us. We would even spend some holidays with friends. That helped a lot! We used to camp with our church friends in Yosemite for a week every summer. Once the family beach trip didn't include us anymore, my parents invited our family friends to rent a beach house with us instead. It was so much fun! By splitting the cost between five families, it was affordable. We'd pack all five families into one beach house and have lots of great times together! Each family had a bedroom. Each mom took turns cooking meals, sometimes we'd eat out. We could body surf, lay in the sand, play games, it was the best! We moved on and made the best of a bad situation. And, of course, I learned that lesson that a person's title doesn't matter. These people were my "family."

The Ever Lovely Junior High

So there were good church friends and even one good school friend. At age 12 I felt like I had a best friend at school for the first time in my life. I'd always survived school with little relational enjoyment (probably because I went to a new school almost every year and sometimes two in the same year). But, in Jr. High I finally had a best friend, and what better time? Jr. High with all its ugliness is made bearable when there's a best friend in the picture, and mine was named Courtney.

Courtney and I laughed and laughed until we couldn't breathe. She was goofy, but could be serious. She was out-of-the box enough that I didn't feel weird marching to the beat of my own drum, too. I'd never been able to be in the box in any way, at any time, so her quirkiness made me feel at home. Courtney was pretty, witty, and smart and we just clicked. It was wonderful (although she frequently had bad breath, but I digress).

One day I went to school and she wasn't at our meeting spot. I was so bummed because break time and lunchtime were difficult without her. The insecurities that rattle you at that age made her absence seem like a catastrophe. I went to class and then had to face break time alone. Then to my delight, as I walked out of my language class, I spotted her! Liberated from the dreadful thought of spending break alone, I sprinted over to her and blurted, "Courtney, you're here! I'm *so* glad! I was wondering what I was going to do!" But she didn't speak. She just kept walking…away…from me. I followed her and kept on saying, "Ha, ha. What are you doing? How was church last night?"

Courtney walked…away from me…and up to another group of girls. I trailed right behind her, curious about this joke she was playing on me. Not one girl in the group, including Courtney, would even look at me. They all kept looking at each other.

When I spoke up to contribute to the conversation, one of them said, "Do you hear an annoying sound?" Another girl confirmed she also heard it. They all smiled at each other as if everything was going exactly as they'd planned. It took me a minute to realize this was *not* a joke. These were the faces of cruelty, a perfect example of mean girls being mean. My "best friend" never spoke to me again that year.

Rejection. Have you felt its sting? I was crushed, completely devastated by that cold-blooded, junior high rejection! I remember how it felt walking away from that circle of girls who'd conspired to injure me. I headed into the bathroom feeling sick to my stomach. Jr. High is such an abominable time of life, for so many reasons. To add this kind of rejection is inhumane.

At the same time, I was in a homeroom class with an abusive teacher. She reiterated my lack of value by putting my desk in a corner when I didn't live up to her expectations. She'd also call me up to get a paper from her and then drop the paper on the floor right as I approached her. She dropped it on purpose so I'd have to bend down and pick up. Then she'd scold me as I was bending down to get the paper. I knew she didn't like me, but I didn't know why. My best friend didn't like me anymore, but I didn't know why either. Rejection, rejection, rejection, and hidden in all these rejections were more invitations.

Learning From the Pain

From the loss of that friendship I learned that I shouldn't put all my friendship eggs in one basket. From that invitation God invited me to learn that it's good to have several friends, not just one main best friend you do everything with. I learned I should never, ever, ever get my value from a person, but from God alone. My worth was not diminished one percent by Courtney's rejection. I also learned how it feels to be on the receiving side of sheer hatefulness. At that point I decided there's never a good reason to be mean; I learned to be kind, no exceptions. Don't you wish that the whole world would learn that lesson?

In light of my junior high pain, my mom called over that close, single, male, family friend of ours who was also a pastor at our church to console and counsel me. Seemed like a good idea at the time, I'm sure. He came, and he did console me. That day he brought consolation. Soon he'd bring sexual advances. Each of those pieces of rejection and then ultimately his immorality brought me more invitations.

When a pastor has a sexual relationship with you when you're in your early teen years, you get an awesome invitation! Through this God invited me to understand in no uncertain terms that He ALONE is God, and that all people are, well, just people. He invited me never to put my faith in a person-EVER! Again, regardless of his title, even if it's "pastor," "prophet," "principal," "CEO," "elder," "parent," whatever, it doesn't matter. There is but ONE GOD, and He is not like man. I was invited to see how God caused me to float out of my body while the pastor defiled me. God covered me with His scarlet blood, so I could walk out of that man's hotel room white as snow. The invitation I was given was to see the difference between man and God. That's a valuable thing to learn. So I accepted the invitation.

I went on through high school without many girlfriends. I found guy friends to be much simpler. Most of them said what they meant. Those I hung with didn't play mind games. If you made them angry, they'd tell you, and then they'd get over it. I loved that! I loved how the male brain thinks; still do! After that "best friend" betrayed me, I never again hung out with girls at school.

I began hanging out with a group of about ten guys, no girls. It was awesome! In that group of ten guys was the guy that would become my beloved, knight-in shining-armor, my dreamy husband. I scored big time when I got him! My relationship with him was just a friendship all through high school. We established an amazing foundation of friendship for four years before we ever dated. That is a fabulous way to start! We've been married for 20 years now, and our relationship just keeps getting sweeter! I adore my husband! If Courtney wouldn't have betrayed me the way she did, I might not have developed the relationship that I did with my husband. Something bitter turned into something sweet. That's God.

We continued to go to the beach and to Yosemite each year with those family friends. We made a lot of good memories in those summer trips. We'd have campfires and barbecued meals, trips down the river or to the boardwalk. My photo albums were lined with pictures of the people who replaced our biological family. We'd have lunch nearly every Sunday after church, and the moms and kids met several times a week for afternoon coffee. One of the ladies had a cappuccino machine that was before its time. This was before Starbucks existed in our city. She could froth and steam the milk just the way they liked it! Being a social butterfly, I thought these frequent gatherings were marvelous. The good and bad, the acceptance and rejection swirling around me. That's life.

Let's Die, Shall We?

My husband and I married when we were babies. We started dating when I was 17, and we got married when we were 20. After we'd been married for just nine months, I was told I'd probably never be able to conceive. I was devastated thinking I might never be a mom. (Obviously, I was able to have children after all, but I almost died in childbirth.)

When I almost died, I was given several invitations. I was invited to value life and *never* take it for granted because it can slip away in the blink of an eye. Through that experience, I became painfully aware I could die at any moment and therefore chose to live life to the full. I was invited to see an angel or Jesus and interact with him and, therefore, have my faith become something even more tangible.

I was invited to become so weak and physically frail that I knew God alone could sustain me. I was invited to understand more deeply that my life was in God's hands, and I was only alive because He chose for me to be alive. The fact that I lived through childbirth was deemed a miracle. So, lastly, I was invited to be a miracle, and I accepted!

Through my not-so-smooth recovery from nearly dying there were lots of visits and gifts from our church family. They continued to take the place of the biological family I wished I had. They were my aunts and uncles and grandparents. People came and prayed for me and cheered me up. Nearly dying and then not recovering well has a way of bumming you out. When the days of recovery turn into weeks, and the weeks turn into months, you tend to get depressed. Through it all, our church family was there. That made all the difference. We weren't alone.

Then, just three months after nearly dying, my parents had

another one of their "financial crashes." One of the five families we were so close with graciously offered for them to move in with them! My little brother, who was getting ready to graduate from high school, moved into our two-bedroom, 900 square foot apartment with my husband and me and our newborn, preemie son.

I'd always tried to hide my family's penniless bank accounts as best I could. Despite my best efforts, our impoverished state seemed to be on display for the whole church to see. These sorts of things have a way of being found out. I often felt as though we'd make our way into the church, sit in our designated pew and then "it" would appear, the scarlet letter, the arrow that hung over us that pointed us out and shouted, "Here they are, the loser, poor family, right here!" I felt judgmental eyes peering into the back of our heads every Sunday. At least we were surrounded by those five families that were our friends no matter what. We'd all sit together in the same section, and that did help. Still, those judgmental eyes behind me could have burned a hole in the back of my head.

In March of 1998 I almost died in childbirth. In May of 1998 Seinfeld ran their final episode ever. In June of 1998 my parents became homeless and my brother moved in with me. Also in June of 1998 my nightmares intensified. I'd always had them, but then I started having them every night. In July of 1998 a friend from Texas came to meet our four-month old son. During her visit I had my first major panic attack and the full-scale onset of post-traumatic-stress syndrome which was a result of nearly dying and a traumatic childhood. At the time I'd never heard about PTS so I thought that I'd lost my ever-loving mind. It was terrifying.

In August of 1998 those five families we'd vacationed with

and who'd replaced our biological family called a meeting. In the meeting three of the five families said in short, "We're not hanging out anymore, but hey, thanks for the memories." They simultaneously tossed over a rubber-banded stack of pictures of us that they no longer wanted, seeing as how we were no longer going to be friends, per their request. This relational casualty proved to be more painful than any of the others.

You're Invited Too!

1998 did not exactly win the "best year ever" award! The only thing that kept me from being suicidal during this year was that I couldn't bear to leave my new son motherless. I also had a deep-seated belief that if God caused to me live, He MUST have a reason, and I should find out what that reason was. Hidden, deep down in the darkest of nights, in the horrors, betrayals, nightmares, near-deaths, panic attacks, and relational abandonments were invitations that had my name on them. They were personalized. They weren't given out to people in general. They were being given to *me*. They were invitations into a deep, personal, intimate, healing relationship with God.

As good as some people might be to us, they will never be God. People will hurt us, some will walk away, worse yet-some will walk away in the *middle* of our darkest night like our family friends did or like the other girls who refused to tell on the pastor. That's not God. That's *people*! God is unwaveringly faithful. If you have ever been maimed by life's cruelties, there is a personalized invitation with your name on it, too. You just have to choose to accept it. I assure you, it will be an invitation to something good. That's just God's way.

When we run to God with our pain, He uses each of these tragic and hurtful situations in our life for something good. Just as He promised, He turned the darkness on its head and made it into something that benefitted me. Each of these losses ultimately resulted in more gains. If I lost five but I gained back thirty-five. What people meant for my harm, God meant for my good. He took each loss and He redeemed it. He's a redeemer by His very nature. As each person walked away, God moved in closer. As people treated me like a liability, He showed me my true value. He's near to the broken-hearted. He's just got a thing for them!

So I accepted His invitations and ended up getting to know Him in a way that many don't. You should always RSVP "YES" to God's personalized invitations. That's the point at which you go from a victim to a blessed and highly favored one. Our acceptance of His invitations is crucial to our seeing redemption begin its priceless process. Accepting His invitation will require you to trust that He was telling the truth when He said, "...in *all things* God works for the good of those who love Him" (Romans 8:28).

If I could go backwards and remove all these hurts from my life, but in turn lose what I gained with God, I wouldn't even consider it. He's everything to me. So at this point all I would do is say, "Hey, God, thanks for the invite!"

Question: Ask God, "What invitation are You extending to me?"

Endnote:

[1] Coldplay. "The Scientist" Recorded 2002. Parlophone (UK) Capitol (US).

CHAPTER 22

Poor Girl, Rich Girl

I don't know why fortune smiles on some and lets the rest go free.[1]

My husband and I and two friends of ours had gone up to a lake that was way off the beaten path. For hours we had to use four-wheel drive to get over these huge boulders in order to reach this lake. The guy that was driving had been to this lake before, and assured us that the beauty of this place would be worth this long, difficult journey. However, once we finally arrived, there was a *total* infestation of mosquitos!

Trying to shoo away the mosquitos was as effective as breathing under water. They were flying into our eyes, noses, mouths, ears, and down our shirts. If they could survive the journey down our windpipes, then there were mosquito bites on our lungs as well. I'd never seen anything like this. I now understood the value of a mosquito net. We were camped at the beautiful glassy lake with enormous trees and rocks surrounding us high in the Sierra Nevada Mountain Range of California. The arresting beauty of the nature that enveloped us could not be appreciated, as we were too busy fighting for our lives.

As much as we swatted and blew and waved our hands in the air like crazy people, we could not keep them from biting us. Our skin was marred from head to toe with the physical evidence of the war we were in, lest there be any doubt. Had we not captured a photograph of the lake and nature, I wouldn't have even remembered what it looked like. All I remembered was the buzz of their wings, the burn of their swelling bites, and the utter exhaustion of *every single second* trying to minimize their damage.

That mosquito infestation is just like the effect that poverty had on my life. Poverty prevents you from being able to see the beauty of life because you are so caught up in the *constant* battle to survive.

Poverty changes who you are. Poverty is a filter through which everything else is seen. Poverty does not compartmentalize itself. It invades every aspect of everything you do, think, feel, and believe. It's a way of living, but it's also a spirit and a mentality. It disfigures your soul. Poverty was birthed in the bowels of hell.

Poverty has cost me several relationships. Not all people are willing to be around the stench that poverty gives off. Poverty has robbed many people of the most basic human dignities. It has kept from me some of what I needed and most of what I wanted. It's most consistently shamed me, and anyone else who has lived within its boundaries for a substantial length of time. Shame and poverty are brother and sister. Perhaps it's possible to be tied to poverty without being tied to shame, but that was not my experience.

The shame of my family's neediness made me try to hide it. Singer/songwriter Paul Simon said, "The poor boy changes clothes and puts on aftershave to compensate for his ordinary shoes." [2] I'd done that. I'd put lipstick on a pig. So much of my life was spent dressing up my poverty to appear to be someone that I wasn't. Why do we do that? Why do we try to present a false self to others so that we'll feel acceptable to them? Have you ever tried to present a forged copy of who you really were so that you'd feel more valuable? Inauthenticity is another unfortunate effect poverty had on me.

Worse than all its other effects, poverty sets children up to be victimized. As if poverty and shame aren't bad enough, they also make a child vulnerable to a variety of predators. I see that now, and I understand why I was victimized over and over and over again. Poverty set the stage for that to be my reality.

I can understand now the role that insufficient funds played in the repetitive savagery that stalked me. When parents are submerged in a battle to swat poverty away and avoid being bitten to death by it, can they really be the guardians they should? Can they get their eyes off their battle long enough to see the lake, trees, and rocks, or the snakes, bears, and lions that are approaching? No, they can't see those things because the divergence of getting their eyes off surviving will cost them too much. Destitution kills one's ability to thrive and backs him into a corner where survival is the only option. It steals choice. It smothers and suffocates and kills the spirit of a person.

I'm always fascinated when people say, "We were poor, but we didn't know it." I was poor, and I sure knew it! I don't even understand that statement. The only thing I can think of is that you might not know you're poor if you're completely surrounded by other poor people, too. Then your poverty might just seem normal. I was always around people that had a lot more money than I did, and I knew it. It sucked as bad as those mosquitos.

Secret Code

I'm pushing "pause" on my story just long enough to tell you a secret. I've been told that only 10% of the people who bought my book will ever *begin* reading it. Only 5% of those people will ever read past the second chapter. Startling statistic, huh? Sooooo, if you're reading this paragraph right now you are the cream of the crop! You're an exceptional type of person that is a true go-getter. Nice job! Do me a favor, if you're reading this right now I want you to message me and tell me this: "I'm the 5%". That way I'll know who has really read this book and who has not. If you tell me that you liked my book, but don't mention that you're the 5% I'll know you haven't really read it.

You can message me on Facebook: Rachel Hamm, or Instagram: rachelhamm29, or email: rachelhamm@att.net Simply type: "I'm the 5%". It will be our little secret. Please don't tell anyone this secret. It's just between me and you. Now back to business...

Everything Changed in the Process

At one point we lost our home to foreclosure. Through a series of bad choices on our part, bad decisions on the part of someone else, events that were outside of our control and a bad economy, we lost the house our kids had loved. I didn't love the house, but I did hate losing it. I hated losing it because it brought even more shame upon me. Because of growing up poor, I was forever trying to prove something to the world around me: I have value...I'm not stupid...I'm not worthless. For most of my life, I felt stupid and worthless largely, but not entirely, because of poverty.

If you didn't grow up in an impoverished home, I don't think you can understand what it does to you. Recovering from the humiliation of the foreclosure was no small thing. I knew logically it was not the end of the world, but it felt like it was. I remember being at a Bible study where a man made a horribly judgmental comment about people who'd "let" their house go to foreclosure. He had no idea we'd just finished ours. I was mortified. I just hoped I could keep it a secret, so I wouldn't be judged any more than I already had been. Why do we judge each other so harshly? There is a time for us to be accountable to one another, but then there's just cold-blooded, arrogant judgement.

To me, poverty felt like an identity more than a situation. When I told on the pastor for his sexually inappropriate behavior, I was told people thought I was doing it just to get money because of how I'd grown up poor. That put a fiery arrow through my already deeply wounded heart. They thought I was seeking money because people saw poverty as being my identity, or at least part of it. I never asked for a dime from the church. Their judgements and assumptions were a reflection of their dark, judgmental hearts. I see that now, but at the time it was so embarrassing and painful to me. That was such a cruel, hurtful, and embarrassing accusation.

It's interesting how much poverty was hardwired into me. After age 22 I wasn't even poor anymore. I grew up poor, and our first two years of marriage were spent in poverty, but after that we were fine. My husband made a good living, and we were not poor. But, I felt poor no matter how much money we had. Poverty had deep roots in my soul. That's why I say it's a spirit. Sometimes poverty is simply a reality. Other times, it's a spirit that needles its way into your soul, regardless of your financial position.

After I entered counseling for the sexual abuse I got over the humiliation of the foreclosure. As I got healing for my deep-seated wounds, that shame/poverty issue just seemed to resolve itself. I went to counseling to deal with my wounds from sexual abuse, but in the process all these other "side note" issues I had were simultaneously healed. It was interesting how things that I thought were separate were actually completely intertwined. It's like the glass on my entire worldview lens was cleaned while in counseling. My healing process made everything look different. I could see things as they really were instead of seeing them as being all mangled and messed up through my unhealthy, smudged up worldview lens.

Please hear me on this next point...when we have untreated emotional wounds, we will have a skewed view of the world around us. We will frame everything we see, feel, and hear from a place of wounded-ness. The world looks, sounds, and feels different when you're lying in the gutter. If you've been lying in the gutter your whole life, then you don't even know that's abnormal. So as I was in the process of getting counseling, everything around me began to look different. It was a wonderful thing.

About ten months after I'd told on that pastor, I was starting to really enjoy some fruits of my labor. I was starting to feel free and healthy on a level I didn't even know was possible. Things that used to hurt my feelings didn't hurt anymore. Shame that I used to wear around my neck was replaced by dignity, peace, and confidence.

ANOTHER MOVE?!

As I'd mentioned, just prior to my entering counseling, we rented another home. Just ten months after we moved in, our landlord informed us he was selling the house and we needed to move. We would have *never* moved into that house had we known he was going to do that. Moving is HORRIBLE, and we'd hoped to stay in that house until we were able to buy again. We were not ready to buy another house at that time, and the thought of having to move to another rental house made me crazy.

Having our landlord tell us we had to move out felt like pain upon pain. We were still dealing with my past, and the pain of being rejected by the church, and all the consequences that ensued, only to now be faced with moving *again*! I was so frustrated that our landlord decided to sell when we'd lived there such a short time. It felt like we'd been through so much already, our hearts were still in repair, and moving again was the last thing we needed.

At that point I began to cry out to God for mercy. I asked Him to begin redeeming the pain and injustice we'd experienced. I asked Him to bless us in direct proportion to how horribly the church had treated us and to bring some balance to our scales. The way that the church handled things and the way they treated us was unacceptable, and I wanted some redemption.

The fact that the church had paid my abuser's full salary and benefits for 18 months while I was personally paying thousands of dollars for counseling was financially unjust. They didn't offer to pay for one penny of my counseling. I'd already found God to be One who redeems this type of thing, so just like the persistent widow mentioned in the Bible I began persistently asking

God to redeem our pain. I asked for that, but as we looked for a place to move I struggled to really believe that He would answer my request. I'd seen Him do it in the past, but because my heart was so raw I was struggling to believe I'd see Him do it again.

We looked and looked and looked for another rental, but every time we'd try to put a deposit on one someone would beat us to it. It was crazy how many times that happened to us! The time was approaching for us to move out, and we still didn't have anywhere to go.

One day I found out that a couple I knew through a mutual friend was selling their house. I'd been to their house for a baby shower, and I'd LOVED their house! It was in an older neighborhood where all the houses had so much charm. Their house was built in 1926, had five bedrooms, a sunroom, and a bright and charming kitchen that had been remodeled in blue (my favorite color). It also had a guest house and a pool! The yard had huge trees, a pond and fountain that was full of fish, and a bird aviary full of finch.

The house was busting at the seams with character, and I was enchanted!

I wondered if they'd consider renting it to us if they couldn't sell it. Because of the foreclosure, we couldn't buy. It seemed like there was no point in telling my husband about this amazing house, since we couldn't buy. But finally, because I couldn't get it out of my head, I showed it to him. He loved it too. We thought the best we could hope for was they might be willing to rent it to us if they couldn't sell it.

CHAPTER 22

You Just Never Know

Then, we found out somehow we qualified to an FHA loan! We were so happy! The amount that we qualified for was low, but we *could* buy a house! Our friends' house was worth $30,000 more than we qualified for. Ultimately, we decided to make an offer for what we could afford. I tracked down the phone number and texted the owner. I told her what price we'd be offering them, and said that we knew the house was worth what they were asking and we didn't want to insult them, but we only qualified for the amount we were offering. She texted back: "We will accept your offer. Can you come over for dinner tonight?"

I was stunned! It seemed so unlikely and then just like that, we got a "yes." I began getting suspicious about why she was so agreeable. Maybe they hadn't sold the house because there's something terribly wrong with it? I felt nervous that there was something we didn't know.

When we went for dinner that night, she said, "I have been praying and praying that a Christian family would buy our house. It felt like kids were supposed to live here, and I really wanted the family that bought our house to be a light in this dark community. This house was originally built by a family who took in orphans. All five bedrooms were filled to the brim with children that had no home and no parents. I believe that God wanted someone of the same spirit to buy the house. You guys fit that criteria, but that's not why we accepted your offer so quickly. There's another reason..."

She continued, "Several months ago we received a full price offer, no contingencies. It seemed like a perfect offer. We were getting ready to sign papers to accept the offer when the Lord spoke to me and told me NOT to accept the offer. It was so strong. I told my husband who was concerned about turning down an offer like that, but he trusted I'd heard from the Lord and we turned it down.

"As we drove home from our realtor's office after having just turned down a full price offer, we were silent. We were thinking, 'What have we just done?'

"When we got home, our girls asked if we could fill up their water balloons. As we were filling them with the hose, a woman walked up to the house. All I could think of was that she was from water code enforcement because they'd been giving fines to people who were watering on the wrong days due to the severe drought. So, I told her we were *not* watering, just filling water balloons. She seemed confused, and I realized she was not from code enforcement. I asked how I could help her. With a strong southern drawl she said, 'Well, it might sound a bit strange, but I believe that the Lord Jesus has sent me to you.'

"I said, 'That doesn't sound strange, but why did He send you?

"The stranger continued, 'Well, it's about the house.'

"'Oh, are you interested in the house? I asked hopefully.

"'No, ma'am.'

"I felt puzzled and said, 'Okay, why are you here?'

"'Well, I believe that the Lord Jesus wanted me to tell you that you are going to receive some offers on your house, but you are to turn them down until you receive an offer from a Christian family He is going to send to buy your house. You are to wait for them to make their offer, and then you are to accept it. You will know when it's the family that God has sent. They will have four sons.'

"My husband and I stood there stunned, jaws on the ground. We just turned down a perfect offer because we *thought* God was telling us to do that, but this was much-needed confirmation. That gave us the fortitude to turn down many more full-price offers and some offers that were *over* their asking price! Then, you submitted your offer, which was $30,000 *below* our asking price, and we accepted it!"

That's the grace of God! I was the victim of injustice with our church. I asked God to vindicate us and bring justice to our scales, and this was the beginning of His saying "yes" to my request. The way we got our beautiful home was a piece of redemption pie. God gave someone instructions in order to bless us, and that's one godly, generous, faithful couple that sacrificed a lot of money to obey the word of the Lord to them. That stranger who gave them that word from the Lord came from Dallas, Texas that day. She didn't even live in this city. She'd obeyed the word of the Lord to her to go to this town in California and deliver that message to total strangers. And our friends had the faith to receive that word and then to obey it.

As for us, we were overwhelmed and received that gift with *grateful* hearts! We love our house so much! It feels like we're surrounded with walls of God's love for us. I literally walk through my house as I go about my day and say out loud, "Thank you, Jesus. Thank for my house. Thank you for this gift. Thank you so much. Thank you."

Our house is so sweet to me. It's got hardwood floors, lots of windows, rose bushes everywhere, huge trees whose branches sprawl over the roof, a sun room, a built-in hutch in the large dining room...it's just lovely. When people come into our house they will often say, "There's something really special about this house," as if they can feel God in it. He's in it for sure. He's in it and His goodness is all over it. He's so generous. He went well beyond what I could have ever hoped for. He gave me more than I deserved. He answered my request to bless us in proportion to how the church had wounded us. That's just who He is. And He was just getting started...

Question: Is there an area of your life where you'd really like to see redemption? Don't just hope that it happens, ask for it. Ask, even if it's your own sins or shortcoming that have caused you the loss that you're wanting to see redeemed.

Endnotes:

1 Henley, Don, Glenn Frey, Joe Walsh, and J.D. Souther. "The Sad Café." Recorded 1978. Asylum.

2 Simon, Paul. "Diamonds on the Souls of her Shoes." Recorded 1987. Warner Bros.

CHAPTER 23

The Desires Of Our Hearts

Delight yourself in the Lord,
and He will give you the desires of your heart.
(Psalm 37:4, ESV)

The Armoire

We moved into our beautiful gift of a home on the first of September, and guess what... it was blazing hot again! Even though this ELEVENTH move was miserably hot, it was still an ideal move into an ideal home. Being an idealist, I found this to be, well ideal.

Because it's an old home, there are little quirks in the house. For instance, there's no coat closet or hall closet. The bedroom closets are tiny, but the rooms are huge. There is very little storage in the whole house.

After draining our savings account to pay for all my counseling, we had to scrape up every dime we had for the down payment down on this house. That meant we had little money to solve the home's issues. For example, in the master bedroom there were two very small closets, but one of them was just an empty space with no rod for hanging clothes and no shelves. We would've liked to have a custom closet organizer made so we could maximize the small space, but decided that would have to wait. We also decided to buy a cheap, used armoire from Craig's List to use in place of a hall closet.

I looked on Craig's List for a used armoire that would be "good enough." I found one that was $150, and it looked decent. I went to look at it, hoping it would work, but the hinges were broken and the wood was peeling. I left disappointed, knowing I'd have stuff piled up on my bedroom floor until I found an armoire; and my mind doesn't handle clutter very well.

On my way home I saw a yard sale sign and, without thinking, like a daydreaming drone I was steered to this yard sale. I don't really go to yard sales much, and I wasn't going to this one with an agenda. I was not even conscious of why I'd turned towards the sale. When I pulled up, there was an armoire right in the middle of the driveway that was better than any I'd seen on Craig's List. I hopped out of my car and jogged over to it, as I'd seen a man also heading to the armoire. I beat him to it, opened the doors and looked it over. I wanted it! So, I approached the owner and asked, "How much for your armoire?" hoping it was going to be an affordable price.

She looked at me and kind of stared into my eyes for a second, then said, "Honey, I feel like the Lord wants me to *give* it to you...for free. God bless you!"

What? Awesome!

We were moving the next day, so we already had a U-Haul. Later in the day we drove it on over to this lady's house to pick up our free armoire. When we got there, she said, "Would you like a child-size redwood picnic table, a large area rug, and a large, brand new ice chest too?" We wanted it all, and she gave it to us, for free.

This free armoire and other goodies seemed like a little bit more redemption. Besides asking God to bring justice to our scales, I've always asked for His favor to rest upon me, and you know what? It does! I'm always looking for where God is leading me. I don't want to miss *anything* He has for me! It's not always easy to follow His leading. His leading often sounds like a small whisper that can be easy to miss, especially if I'm overly busy. I think being overly busy is one of the main things that keeps us from God's best for us. So, I fight to keep my schedule from being too full. I also ask God to anoint my ears to hear His most gentle of whispers. He does.

The Clothing Rack

A few days after we moved with our armoire in tow, I was driving home from my counselor's office, thinking about what we could do with the empty space in that closet until we could afford to have the custom organizer made. I suddenly remembered I could buy free-standing clothing racks until we could do something customized.

I decided to check Lowe's or Target the next day for a free-standing clothing rack. No sooner did I have that thought when I saw a free-standing clothing rack on the side of the street with a sign on it that said, "FOR RACHEL."

What. In. The. World? I quickly pulled over and looked at the rack, and it was just what I needed. I ran up and knocked on the front door of the house. A lovely Hispanic woman around 50 years old opened the door. I asked her if her clothing rack was for sale. She said, "No, why? Do you want it?" I said yes, and she told me I could have it for free. Then she came out to help me load it into my car.

My curiosity got the best of me and I had to ask why in the world the sign on it says, "FOR RACHEL." She said, "Oh, my sister-in-law's name is Rachel, and I was just using that clothing rack as a sign holder because the chair next to it is for her. And you know what's funny? My name is Rachel, too!"

I said, "*Well, my name is Rachel, too*, and I need a clothing rack!" She laughed and said, "Well, I think God wants *you* to have it!"

She helped me load it into my car and off I went with my free clothing rack with the sign still hanging on it, "FOR RACHEL!" I marveled at the way God went about giving that to me. He's so creative! For those who have eyes to see, He's creating gifts and experiences for us all around. As small as this gift was, it seemed to me to be another small slice of redemption pie.

Football Camp

A few months later I was taking our youngest son Ezekiel to football camp. The head football coach for our local high school was hosting a football camp for third through sixth graders. Ezekiel was in third grade, and he was so excited that he was finally old enough to go to this camp! Besides loving football, he was excited because this head coach used to play in the NFL and, in fact, had won a Super Bowl with the Colts.

As we drove to camp, Ezekiel said, "I'm so excited about this, Mom! Do you understand that I'm going to be learning to play football from a *real* NFL player? Do you know how cool that is? I just hope that I actually get to meet him and shake his hand. That would be great, *a real NFL player!* They're going to be giving out some prizes too, and I really hope that I get one!"

I asked what the prizes were for, and Ezekiel explained that kids who stood out as doing a great job would be rewarded for their exceptional effort.

I replied with a prayer, "Well, God, I pray that Zeke *will* get to meet this coach. I pray that Your favor will rest on him and that he'll get one of the prizes also. I pray that You'll protect him, bless him, and help him to stand out among all the other boys as he gives 110% today."

"Thanks, Mom. I have a good feeling that all of that will happen."

"I hope so, buddy." I told him.

When we arrived at camp, I walked Zeke up to the registration table, and no one else was in line. I said to the person checking in the kids, "This is Ezekiel Hamm and he's pre-registered."

As soon I said that to the registrar, we heard, "Ezekiel Hamm? Ezekiel, that is such a cool name! I love that name!" We turned to see that NFL player, now head coach, standing there with his hand extended out to shake Ezekiel's. Ezekiel blushed as he extended his hand right back.

"Thank you. Nice to meet you," Ezekiel said. He turned to me with a look of pure joy on his face. "Mom, that was *him*!"

"I know! That's awesome. Thank you, God!" I whispered into

his ear. He winked at me and sprinted onto the field to join the other kids. I drove away with a thankful heart that Ezekiel just got a desire of his heart. It felt so wonderful to see my child have the favor of the Lord on him. It's one of the best feelings in the world!

When camp was over, I saw him walking toward me wearing a new hat, with a snow cone in hand, and a smile on his face.

"Guess what? I got one of the prizes! The coaching staff was watching the players all through camp and at that end they gave away six hats to the six kids that had stood out for doing a great job and for giving it all we've got, and *I got one!*" There were about 75 players at the football camp, so getting one of the six hats was quite an achievement.

After I celebrated with Ezekiel and told him how proud I was of him for being one of the hardest workers there, I explained that God had favored him. "We can work hard and no one notice it. You got that hat because you worked hard, yes, but you also got that hat because God's favor was on you. God's favor caused the coaches to be looking at you at just the right times so they'd see you at your best. That's God's favor!"

He agreed, and we prayed a prayer of thanksgiving for God's goodness to us.

Ezekiel right after football camp

Who Knew There Were Vacuum Miracles?

A few months later the school year was coming to an end which meant that our oldest son Jackson would be graduating from high school and leaving home. He was a great kid, with a good head on his shoulders and a heart for the Lord. He was going to participate in a missions program called Youth With A Mission (Y.W.A.M.), and we were thrilled about his decision to do that. I had total peace about him moving into manhood and going to Y.W.A.M., but that didn't eliminate the sadness that a mom feels when her son is preparing to leave home.

I was throwing him a graduation party at our house and there was a lot to do to prepare for that. For one, I needed to clean the house, but when I went to use the vacuum, it was broken. I already had more on my "to do" list than I could possibly get done, and I was overwhelmed. I did not have time for the vacuum to break! I was battling with all that had to be done physically to prepare for the party, but most of my struggle was the grief I felt about our son leaving home.

So, with much frustration I loaded up the vacuum and headed to the vacuum repair shop, which was a good 20 minutes from our house. I got to the shop and couldn't find a parking place anywhere! I finally parked a block away and had to lug my vacuum and all its accessories back to the shop. It was 102 degrees out, literally, and I was miserable, emotional, and on edge. I finally got to the door and there was a note on it that read, "Closed for a family vacation."

I lost it. I began crying (and probably talking to myself) as I drug the vacuum stuff back down the block. I threw it all in my trunk and cried the whole way home. Now those tears were mostly "my son is going far, far away, and I'm sad about that" tears, but the vacuum being broken and now unable to be fixed didn't help at all.

The next morning my husband came in to tell me goodbye as he was leaving for work. He took one look at me and asked me what was wrong. I told him about the vacuum situation and how I just wanted everything to be perfect for Jackson's party. As I talked I began to cry again, and I'm not an emotional person. Marshall came over, put his arms around me, and began to pray for me. I felt some relief as he prayed. We said goodbye and he left for work.

About 30 seconds after he walked out the front door, he walked back in and said, "Do you know why there's a vacuum on our walkway?" I asked him if it was ours as I thought maybe I'd forgotten to bring it. He said it was not our vacuum. We headed back out the front door and sure enough, there was a vacuum sitting there just staring at us. We turned and looked at each other and knew immediately that something special was happening. Marshall asked me who knew that our vacuum was broken. I told him I had not told one single soul. Absolutely no one knew. Just to be certain, we asked all our neighbors if it belonged to them. They all said it did not.

God knew I needed a vacuum. God knew my heart was hurting. God knew that I really wanted to clean my house and have it "just so" for the party. God knew I was a mom grieving her son's leaving. In that moment I didn't need food or money or a car. I needed a vacuum, so God delivered one.

As weird as it may sound, this miracle is one of my favorites. It showed me that God cares about everything that concerns us, *everything*. When I brought that vacuum into my home that day, it felt like God was saying, "I see you. I'm with you. I've got you. I love you."

It may not seem like getting a vacuum would be part of bringing justice to my scales, but it was. The *way* that I got the vacuum allowed me to receive new revelation of who God is and how much He cares about us. Revelation about God is my favorite thing in the whole world. God knows that nothing thrills me more than His miraculous activity in my life. So, by giving me that vacuum in that particular way, He was giving me the desire of my heart. That feels like redemption and justice to me.

Dreams Really Do Come True

"It's the possibility of having a dream come true that makes life interesting." [1]

I've tried to train our sons to look for God. I'm always pointing things out and saying, "That's God!" as I teach them His ways. All four of our sons have a heart for the Lord. When I read about David and Joseph in the Bible, I often see my son Ethan as having a similar anointing as them. He's got a pure heart. He's creative. He's a dreamer. He's handsome, and most of all he's sweet.

I'd been telling Ethan I thought he was a prophetic dreamer, but he didn't think so. He thought I put too much weight on dreams, and he wasn't convinced they mattered much.

A few months after moving into our amazing home, Ethan woke up and said he had a dream he'd met Keith Urban. I said maybe he would be meeting him someday. We moved on and didn't think much of it.

About a week later he dreamed it again. He said, "I had AN-OTHER dream last night that I met Keith Urban." Keith Urban is Ethan's favorite musician, so I knew there was a chance his dreams were just showing the desire of his heart, and might not be prophetic. I simply said I hoped he did get to meet Keith. Then I asked God to make a way for that to happen *if it was supposed to.* Once again I moved on, not thinking much of it. I saw no possible way that was going to happen, so it was easy to forget about it.

A few weeks later, I received an email from "American Idol" offering me tickets to be in their live audience. It was the last season of "American Idol," so I'd signed up to get tickets. They had a lottery system where you could submit your name, and possibly be chosen to receive tickets.

My friend Tami, my sons Ethan and Jonah, and I drove to L.A. to go to the show. We knew we had to get there early because having a ticket only gives you a *chance* to get into the show; it's not a guarantee. So we got there around 10:45 AM, and the doors opened at 2:30 PM. We were numbers 16, 17, 18, and 19 in line, so we thought we'd definitely get in.

We STOOD in line from 10:45 until 2:30. That's when the man from "American Idol" said they *only had seats for* the first 20 people in line. I turned to look at the line behind us. There were probably 300 to 400 people in line that *had tickets* but did *not* get in. We got in, just barely; but barely counts.

At "American Idol" they allow all the teenagers to stand around the stage, while the adults sit in the seats. Jonah did not want to stand at the stage, especially after all those hours of standing in line. So the boys were going to sit with Tami and me, but when we got to the door, they said all teenagers *had* to stand at the stage. So, Ethan and Jonah were off to the stage for several more hours of standing.

As they were ready to start filming, the doors opened and in walked the judges, Harry, Jennifer, and Mr. Keith Urban. There were some teen girls standing near Ethan and Jonah who were screaming for Keith to come to them. He walked over and shook lots of hands with the kids all along the stage. Ethan, who is small for his age, was standing behind all these tall, screaming girls. He must have been a foot shorter than they were, and he was completely swallowed up by the sea of taller, screaming kids.

Keith finished greeting kids and turned to walk to his seat. Then, out of nowhere, he stopped dead in his tracks and whipped himself back around quickly, as if something or someone stopped him and told him to go back. Keith walked back over to the edge of the stage and lifted his head up as if he were looking over all the taller kids, then he pointed at Ethan. Keith motioned for Ethan to come to him. Ethan had a look on his face that said, "Who? Me?" He timidly took a step towards Keith, but Keith reached through the crowd and grabbed Ethan's hand and pulled him all the way up to himself. He introduced himself to Ethan, and asked if he'd like to take a picture with him. Ethan excitedly said, "Yes!" They shook hands and Keith said, "Nice to meet you, brother." And just like that, Ethan's dreams came true, literally. *That's God.*

As Tami and I stood in that "American Idol" balcony watching all of this unfold for Ethan, as if in slow motion, my body buzzed with euphoria! I knew what that meant to Ethan. I knew he'd longed to meet Keith Urban and had his whole year made by the favor that God and Keith had just shown him. I knew God showed Ethan this was going to be happening through his two dreams. I was beside myself with excitement. Ethan tasted the wild honey with a look of pure satisfaction.

And then God spoke to me, "Precious, Rachel, as you watch this happen for Ethan you are feeling what is in My heart. I LOVE to give my children the desires of their hearts! I LOVE to give my children favor! I LOVE to give my children divine appointments! I LOVE to give my children gifts! The joy you feel seeing this happen for Ethan is the joy I have as I watch My children walk into the divine appointments I've set up for them.

"It gives me great joy when I see a child of Mine whose spirit and eyes are open enough for Me to lead them to the gifts I have for them. I am not withholding anything from My children the way many think I am. Quite the opposite. I have so many gifts stored up for My children, so many divine appointments, so much favor. I just wait for them to turn their eyes and ears toward Me, so I can lead them to the wildly satiating honey. *That is My heart."*

Jonah Hamm is to the left, Ethan Hamm, and Keith Urban

After "American Idol" we drove back from Los Angeles. My friend Tami was taking a turn driving, and we had Kenny Chesney playing on the radio. I was looking out my side window and up at the stars, thanking God for the star Ethan met. I was just worshipping God for His sweetness towards my family. That's when God said, "You're so welcome, but you haven't even noticed the date yet." I quickly grabbed my phone and clicked on the button that lights up my home screen. The date: 3-17. A rush of exhilaration flooded my heart and tears brimmed my eyes. 317, *again*.

Besides a ton of gratitude, I also thought, God is so fun. He's just a creative blast. Following His leading makes my life exhilarating! Then, I felt sad thinking about how misunderstood He is. So many people who don't know Him or don't know Him well think He's boring. They've never veered off the path of the masses to get to where the wild honey is. I felt grieved that they could be so wrong about who He really is.

In that moment I felt the Lord say, "As you've been so misunderstood your whole life, you've shared in My sufferings. I am so misunderstood. As you've been rejected by the religious people, you've become acquainted with how I was treated by religious people when I walked the earth. As people in your life have betrayed you, you've developed more of My heart. You're in good company, Rachel, and great is your reward in heaven!" As we flew down that stretch of darkened highway, I sat in the joy of knowing I was completely understood by the One who is misunderstood.

Music

You may have noticed that I quote a lot of song lyrics in this book. I'm a life-long impassioned music-lover. Music takes me away like none other. I love musicians, writers, singers, amps, instruments, speakers, microphones, concerts, I love it all. I can't imagine living without music.

My love for music and people made me a natural fit for a volunteer position hosting Christian artists when they came to perform in our city. My friend, who'd been doing the job, was moving to Nashville and wanted to know if I'd like to take his spot here in California. So I began volunteering for a Christian concert promoter. I'd work from 8:30 AM to midnight and didn't feel like I'd worked for one minute. How could I call it work when I was enjoying myself so much?

I loved this volunteer position so much that I decided that I'd like to get hired by Live Nation, the biggest concert promoter in the world. I looked into it, but month after month there weren't any positions that I'd be interested in. I eventually stopped looking.

One day as I was breezing through our arena a man stopped me. He began asking me questions like, "Do you get star-struck? Do you feel intimidated to drive famous people around?" I assured him that I did not, and that famous people are just people. They're people whom I have a lot of compassion for. This man asked me a few more questions and then said, "I'm a headhunter for Live Nation, and I would like you to work for me as an artist host/runner."

I told him that I'd tried to find a job like this with Live Nation, but couldn't. He said that's because they don't advertise these positions. If you work directly with the artists they find you, you don't find them. This position requires a unique set of traits and they're very picky about who does this job. I was thrilled, filled out the paperwork, had some training, and went to work for the largest concert promoter on the planet.

I love my job! I get to listen to the best musicians in the world rehearse and do sound checks, and I'm paid to attend concerts! I meet interesting people from all over the world. I get to love on artists, listen to them, pray for them, and be a blessing to them while they're in my town. Every time I'm at work the scent of honey permeates the arena. Sometimes I have to pinch myself because my job is so wonderful! I can't believe that I get paid to do what I used to happily do for free. My job with Live Nation (and now all the promoters) feels redemptive. It's a gift.

The other night I was at work hosting one of the largest artists in the world. If I said his name, you'd know him. The president and one of the founders of Live Nation had flown in to meet with him and tell him thank you for choosing Live Nation to be his promoter and to congratulate him on a monumental anniversary as a performer. After the founder/president met with the artist, I took him back to his hotel. I got to spend time with this legend in the music industry. He was kind, intelligent, and interesting. He told me that he'd spent time doing each of the positions within his company, Live Nation, and that the position I held was his favorite. He said that he hoped I liked and appreciated my job. I was thankful for the opportunity to tell him how much I cherished my job. As I dropped him off at his hotel I looked up to heaven and said, "Thank you! *I love my life!* Thank you for redemption."

Wait, what?

"Tell your heart that the fear of suffering is worse than the suffering itself. And that no heart has ever suffered when it goes in search of its dreams, because every second of the search is a second's encounter with God and with eternity." [2]

Ethan had another dream that seemed prophetic to me, and at least part of the dream appeared to be about our friend Rick. Rick asked if he could meet Ethan and me so Ethan could tell him the dream. We agreed and met at the café near our house.

Ethan shared the part of the dream that was about Rick, but then he kept going and shared the whole dream. The rest of the dream was about Keith Urban and Nicole Kidman.

I figured that Rick must have been thinking that the part about Keith and Nicole seemed so random, and I wanted to hurry and explain some things to him, but the second Ethan finished recounting his dream, Rick asked, "Are you friends with Keith and Nicole?" Ethan explained that we are not friends with them, but that we have a lot of dreams about them, God shows us things about them, and that our family prays for them *a lot.* He explained that he'd met him briefly at American Idol, but that we don't have a relationship with them. I then added that several years ago the Lord started showing me things about Keith and Nicole before they happened. For instance, God showed me ahead of time that both of their dads were going to die. Both of their dads died a few days *after* the Lord showed me they were going to. There are many things He's shown me about them before they happened, and I would then pray for them. Some of the things He's shown me about Keith and Nicole haven't happened yet. It's been a wild ride to see how we've dreamed things and then we see them play out in their real lives. My family and close friends all know about this quirky prophetic thing with our family and Keith and Nicole. I'm not totally sure why it happens, but I've always seen it as a call to pray for them. So I do, all the time.

Rick listened intently as we explained all this. Then, he said, "That's interesting. Maybe I should set up a meeting with you and them." Wait, what? At first I thought I'd misheard him, but then I looked down at that amber-colored café table the three of us were sharing. Sure enough, dripping with wild honey.

For The Blameless Heart

You might find God on a football field, at a yard sale, when driving down the street, while walking through your local arena, sitting in a coffee shop, or at "American Idol." Keep your eyes open, sweet thing! You never know where you'll run into Him or one of His gifts. Ask Him for favor. Ask Him for divine appointments. Ask Him to help you see His activity around you. God wants to be found. He wants to heal you, give you favor, and set you on the course to your promised land; and we've *all* got a promised land.

I was a poor, broken, wounded girl. I am now a healed, whole, blessed woman who has found God over and over, and usually not where I was expecting to. As I went through my healing process, I began to receive more of what I asked God for. Maybe because the healthier I was, the healthier my requests were. I asked Him for redemption, and He gave it to me. I continuously ask Him to give my family favor, and He does. That's who He is. He is The Giver, Healer, Redeemer. He's restored my dignity, set my feet on solid ground, and showed me how to walk in His ways. My soul is healed. My mind is at peace, and there's abundant joy in my spirit. I asked Him for all of that. Ask Him for whatever it is you need. He's listening, and His eyes are on you.

"For the eyes of the Lord run to and fro throughout the whole earth, to give strong support to those whose heart is blameless toward him."
(2 Chronicles 16:9, ESV)

That's God.

As I wrote the last few words of this book, I felt like the Lord told me to type this verse out for you because this is what He wants to do for you. It's the verse that has been going through my mind the whole time I've been writing:

"And I have promised to bring you up out of your misery... into...a land flowing with milk and honey."

That's what God wants to do for *EVERYONE*. He wants to bring you out of your misery (heal you) and lead you into your promised land (cause you to live the life you were created to live) and bless you abundantly. So I typed that verse out for you, but I wasn't sure where it was located in the Bible. So I looked up the verse and guess what? It was *317 AGAIN!* That verse is found in Exodus 3:17, NIV!

A God-led, honey-filled life is the most exhilarating treasure hunt ever! You won't be bored when you follow God's leading. When we get our wounds healed and when we experience the supernatural life, we are truly fulfilled. We can truly enjoy our life and live it to the full. For me, getting healed and walking closely with God hasn't been life-changing. It's been *life-beginning*.

Question: Do you know God, Jesus, and The Holy Spirit intimately? Your most fulfilled, peaceful, joyful life is on the other side of your healing and in close relationship with The Healer. I promise you, if you haven't gotten healing for your wounds and if you aren't in close relationship with The Father, Son, and Holy Spirit, you're not fully living the life you were created to live. You were created for a promised land!

Endnotes:

1 Coelho, Paulo. *The Alchemist*. New York: HarperCollins, 1998.

2 Ibid.

Made in the USA
Coppell, TX
14 August 2020